Do You

truly

Know Him?

Or Just Know *about* Him?

Journal

Wyatt & Sons Publishers books may be ordered through booksellers or by contacting:

Wyatt & Sons Publishers, LLC
Mobile, Alabama 36695
www.wyattpublishing.com
editor@wyattpublishing.com

Because of the dynamic nature of the Internet, any web address or links contained in this book may have changed since publication and may no longer be valid.

Unless otherwise indicated, all scripture references are Scripture taken from the New King James Version® Copyright ©1982 by Thomas Nelson. Used by permission. All rights reserved.

Cover illustration: Jessica Smith
Cover design by: Sam Noerr
Interior design by: Mark Wyatt

ISBN 13:978-1-954798-26-7
Printed in the United States of America

Do You *truly* Know Him?

Or Just Know *about* Him?

Journal

by

Matcine Pepper

WS

WYATT & SONS
PUBLISHERS, LLC

Mobile, Alabama

TABLE OF CONTENTS

Acknowledgments 7

What People Are Saying About This Book 11

Instructions For The Reader 13

SECTION I: IN THE BEGINNING 15

1   A Man's Heart Plans His Way/Unconditional Love   17
2   Be As Wise As A Serpent   19
3   Who Am I That You Are Mindful Of Me   21
4   Many Are The Afflictions Of The Righteous   25
5   My Testimony Of Hope Restored   27
6   Posture Your Heart   30
7   Reveal Anything In My Heart That Is Not Of You   33
8   Saved From My Sin   35
9   Submit To God   37
10   Thank You For Making A Way Of Escape   40
11   Your Birth Gave Me Life And Purpose   43

Section II: JOURNEY TO WHOLENESS 47

1   A New Life Has Begun   48
2   A Prayer To Abide In God   51
3   Awaken You Who Slumber   54
4   Don't Conform, Be Transformed   57
5   Dwell And Abide   60
6   Illuminate All Darkness   63
7   In My Weakness You Are Made Strong   65
8   Obedience Is Better Than Sacrifice   68
9   The Lord Of The Ring   71
10   Wait Upon The Lord   74
11   Your Love Knows No Bounds   77

Section III: SALVATION, DELIVERANCE AND FREEDOM   81

1   A Light Will Shine   82

2   Do You Know The Resurrection   85

3   Don't Let Your Heart Be Troubled   88

4   He Who Promised Is Faithful   91

5   Holy Spirit, Help Those Who Are Hurting Learn How To Trust You   94

6   Lord, Please Open My Eyes   98

7   New Home And Job Loss Testimony   101

8   Ready Or Not, He's Coming Soon   104

9   The Good Shepherd   107

10   Do You Truly Know Him   110

FINAL THOUGHTS   113

ACKNOWLEDGMENTS

First and foremost, I would like to thank my Heavenly Father, for His patience, unconditional love, and for His Spirit who dwells in me, who helps me live and move and have my being in Him. Without God's love in my life, this book would never have come into being. He birthed it in me before the foundations of the earth.

Now, it is obvious why my life was always such a struggle and seemed hopeless. But, the Greater One who lives in me saw that I was never defeated and He will never let me fail.

As I have grown to know Him more intimately over the last few years, I can see that these messages He put in my heart to share were messages from His heart to mine, but also messages to share with every person destined to read this book. He not only wants me to know how much he loves me, but for all to know how much he loves us, and how far He will go to grow us up in our faith and our relationships with Him.

He is an intentional God; nothing takes place by mistake. The one thing He wants from us once we receive Him as the Lord of our lives is to surrender to Him. When we are surrendered and no longer seeking our will; when our hearts are opened to what He desires for us; being teachable, humble, and willing to die to self, the possibilities with God are limitless.

You will then discover gifts and talents you may have never known you had, or you will focus on sharpening the ones you know about. His gifts are always Kingdom-oriented. He blesses us to be a blessing to others so that they too can have hope, seeing that His love is boundless and filled with much more than we could ever ask or think of. He knows the plans He has for us, and as we yield our lives to Him, we will walk with Him in a way we never knew was possible; fulfilling and being fulfilled. That is what a life in Christ will do for you when you finally understand what it means to truly know Him, and no longer just know about Him. I love You, Jesus!

I would also like to thank my husband, Harvey. Ever since God revealed to me that I was to write a book, he has stood by my side to support me. There have been many ups and downs during this process; times of discouragement from setbacks, and many exciting milestones, as I've had to learn the ins and outs of book writing. These experiences have been valuable lessons and brought us excitement and joy, in the setbacks and delays. At the end of the day no matter what we faced, he stood by my side and covered me in prayer through every challenge before us. Thank you, Harvey, for standing by my side. I love you!

The next person in my heart to thank is my spiritual mother and mentor, Sherry. Without her love, prayers, obedience, commitment to God first, and belief in me when I didn't believe in myself, this book would likely never have happened. She helped to nurture me spiritually during one of the darkest times of my life. She gave me Holy Ghost CPR and helped to jumpstart my empty and dying heart.

After helping me discover I didn't truly know Him, I repented of my sin and recommitted my heart to Jesus. I have journeyed with Him closer in my walk since; learning who He is in me, and who I am in Him. Thank you, Sherry, for loving me as a daughter and teaching by example how to be free in Jesus. Thank you for the countless prayers, and unconditional love; for correcting and rebuking me when I need it; for the many ways you show you care for and love me as Jesus does; for holding me accountable, and for not backing down or compromising on anything. Thank you for the many laughs and the many tears we've shared. Thank you for being my sounding board and allowing me to share my life with you; for always encouraging me to look to Jesus for what concerns me regarding my family, this book, and many other concerns.

I am eternally grateful to God for knitting our hearts together and for you pointing me to Him always; for helping me to see He has a plan for my life. I give Him all of the glory for what He has done. Thank you for being the yielded and obedient vessel He chose to use, so His plan and purpose for my life could begin to take root and blossom to its fullness. Everyone needs a mentor who is so selfless to sow into their lives. May He bless you above and beyond all you can ask or think of! I love you!

My amazing and beautiful book coach and now precious friend, Rae Lynne Johnson, thank you! The many hours of Zoom calls and for your expertise in writing and understanding the ins and outs of making a good book exceptional thank you; for always greeting me with a smile and a heart that genuinely cares about her clients, thank you; for beginning and ending most every meeting in prayer and for seeing God in the big and little achievements, thank you; for being patient, encouraging, understanding, gentle yet firm; for going the extra mile for me when you did not have to, thank you; for making the time to edit in your already busy schedule, and for pointing out to me that I was over-using exclamation marks, thank you!! Sorry, I couldn't resist! LOL

This whole project has been quite an experience for me, and I will always cherish the time God used you in such an impactful way in my life. You are truly a treasure to rising writers and a blessing in my life personally. I am beyond thankful for God sending you to me as I searched for someone to help me make His plan for this book happen.

I look forward to hugging your neck soon, should Jesus tarry. I could say much more, but this forward has already turned into another book, and there are still others to thank. I love you!

I would like to give special thanks to Jessica Smith, the amazing artist who sketched and charcoaled the beautiful cover photo of Jesus. I never imagined when I won an auction for the drawing of this breathtaking piece of art on social media, I would be using it for the cover of this book. God was overseeing every step of this book, and I remember Him clearly saying, "This is your book cover" after it arrived in the mail. I am blessed and honored to be the vessel He chose to make this book happen. But, without the anointed and gifted talent of Jessica Smith, this book would not have its intended effect on those who are destined to read it.

Thank you, Jessica, for allowing me the honor of using the beautiful picture of Jesus for my book. Your hand in this will touch many lives beyond anything you or I can imagine. I pray those who appreciate your gift will search you out on Facebook, or Etsy at:(JessicaSmithArtShop.Etsy.com), and that you will flourish in all that you give your hands to, to the glory of God. Many blessings to you and your precious family. You are loved.

I would also like to give photo credit to Terry Windquist. Thank you for offering to take my bio photo when I first mentioned that I was writing a book. Your offer blessed me and I was thankful when I could take you up on it. Choosing the best photo was hard, but I think I made the right choice. It was a fun time and I am blessed and honored that you took time out of your schedule to do that for me. I highly recommend anyone looking for a wonderful photographer to look you up. I love you!

I would like to give a big shout out to Sam Noerr for his graphic artistic abilities. After me expressing to you what I was looking for, you ran with it and did not disappoint, whatsoever. As much as the title of the book is important, I wanted the face of Jesus to be the main focus and for nothing to draw the eyes away from Him. As the whole purpose of this book is to make people question, *Do I Truly Know Him? Or just know about Him?* The textured cover and the simple lined frame as well as the font selection is perfect! Thank you sir, I believe in my heart, Jesus is going to be proud of the whole outcome of this amazing work.

And finally, last but certainly not least, many other special people have supported, encouraged, and prayed for me during this writing journey:

I would like to thank Angela for standing by me through all of the ups and downs of this writing experience. For praying for me and encouraging me even while you were battling with serious health issues. Thank you for always believing in me and never giving up on me. I love you!

I am thankful for my beautiful niece, Lori, for all of your support, love, and help around my house, and yard; for letting me share many of my writings with you, and for your sharp eye for editing and finding mistakes to help this book be the best it can be. Thank you for loving me and for believing in me! Thank you also for letting me use your printer for my manuscript. I am honored to call you my niece and my sister in Christ! I am blessed watching you flourish with God in your life, and I can hardly wait to see all He has in store for you. Thank you for standing by my side through this writing journey. Keep sowing into others lives and He will bless you in ways you never imagined He would. I love you!

Thank you, to my sister, Mary Alice. Thank you for your prayers, love, and support, as you have been my #1 supporter over the years where my writings are concerned. The apple didn't fall far from the tree, because you, my sister (not by blood only, but in Christ too), have quite a gift to write and to express God's heart. I pray you will consider taking some special time to write more and see how God inspires you. Do it for His glory. This is a gift He gave us both. I know you will fully grasp His purpose for creating you before the earth was formed or came into existence when you start writing what's in His heart. I love you!

I would also like to thank Elaine, Susan, and Sherry, for encouraging me to write God's book. It took me a little while to grasp that He had placed a book in me, but with your help, I finally saw it! Thank you for believing in me and praying during this challenging but rewarding journey. I am forever grateful for your love, prayers, support, and your friendship in Christ. I love each of you dearly.

Special thank you goes to Mark Wyatt, of Wyatt & Sons Publishers, LLC. Mark has been a friend for about fifteen years. I was first introduced to him as a pastor, as I searched for a church open to allowing the Holy Spirit to move; one that operated in signs, wonders, and miracles. This church checked all of our boxes, and then some. He had a way of preaching and teaching the Word of God in a way that makes you hungry for more. We both had roots that started in another local church but didn't know each other then. He is very gifted, creative, and has a great imagination. He has a heart for God and those who need to experience his love. He is married to his beautiful wife, Mary Ann, and they have 4 children, a son and daughter-in-law, and 3 precious grandsons.

If anyone is writing a book and needs a publisher who will handle their manuscript with the utmost care, be efficient, and have their book ready for print in a reasonable time, I highly recommend Wyatt and Sons Publishers.

Thank you, Carol Williams, for helping to edit the devotional portion of the book. Your willingness and heart to help blessed me and I appreciate your kindness. May God richly bless you and all that you put your hands to. I love you.

There are many others to thank, but I cannot thank everyone without leaving someone out. If you prayed for me during these last two years for God's wisdom, guidance, protection, or provision, or any other reason; if you offered me an encouraging word, a hug, or a blessing, you know who you are, and from the bottom of my heart, I say, thank you. You are all loved and so much appreciated.

I pray this book will bless each of you, and thank God for the special place you each hold in my heart. I also pray for all who will set aside time to read this devotional book and work the journal, that your hearts will be blessed beyond anything you expected it could be. God's heart is for you and He longs to have a deep, intimate relationship with each of us. This book, if read as it needs to be, will help you to achieve this desire the Father has for you, and in turn will cause you to walk in His fullness, for the remainder of your days on earth. You will then walk in full assurance of being able to say, Yes, I Truly Know Him! God bless you. You are loved!

What people are saying about the book

DoYou Truly Know Him?
or Just Know *About* Him?...

"God's grace for Matcine shines through her book. As her journey of affliction echoes through her words, it is evident how she daily walked down a very personal and abiding love with the Father.

Each chapter is an opportunity for the reader to draw closer to God through self-reflection, self-honesty, and self-transparency.

I encourage everyone no matter where they are on their journey with God, to dive deep into this book with the expectation that their walk with God will grow deeper and wider than ever before."

—*Ellis Noone*

"This journal is truly from the heart of the Father, through this author's once-shattered life. She was transformed into a beautiful butterfly. When God finished His work in her, she became a most beautiful pearl made by God's healing hands as a gift to us.

Through God's will, this book was birthed, so that we could be restored to the truth of who Father really is in the new birth; we will come to know Him and not just about Him.

I promise you, Holy Spirit will refine you to come to a place within, that you will honestly know Him in such intimacy that you will become just like Him. Yes exactly like He intended.

Through these wonderful writings, you will be healed in your heart, mind, soul, emotions, and spirit.

Be blessed and learn who you are in Christ, and then you can say, yes, I know You, Jesus."

—*Sherry Primley*

"'Do you truly know Him?'

What a question! Loaded, no doubt. Thought-provoking, offensive, scandalous even, is this five-word sentence. Matcine Pepper has not only lived through an amazing journey to answer this question herself, but she has gifted the readers of this wonderfully written and well-laid-out devotional with an incredible opportunity to go deeper within themselves to find out the truth about how well they truly know God.

As the author and guide of this book, Mrs. Pepper shares her testimony of her need for answers and the questions that she asked God during one of the lowest points of her life, which led her on a mission to find out more about her Creator and the many facets He possesses.

Her quest culminated with amazing revelations, a relationship with the Father she'd always dreamed of, and a deep desire to help others who were also questioning God and looking for the same answers.

This devotional will challenge you, awaken you, and create a deeper hunger and thirst for God as you journal your thoughts and press into His arms like never before. By the time you reach the last page, you'll be closer to God than ever and eager to share your experiences with others as the writer has! Get ready to go deeper and truly KNOW God."

—*Tracie Mark Smith, Chaplain*
Recovery Coach/Teacher

"As I began to move through this devotional/journal I soon realized it read more like a 'Field Manual' for all who desire to draw closer in their relationship with God.

Beautifully and thoughtfully written, "Do You Truly Know Him" is a foundational study and reminder of God's prevailing word and presence in our lives. The personal testimonies written with such transparency and the transformative scriptures reminding us of God's majesty and love, no doubt set the reader on a sure and faithful path in deepening their relationship with God.

I highly recommend this devotional for all who seek to know HIM in a deeper and more abiding way. May Holy Spirit touch each of us as we scour over the divinely inspired pages of this instructional 'Field Manual'. May many students of the word pick this up and become more intimate with the knowledge of the Almighty."

—*Mrs. Tami Lightfoot*
Co-Founder, Victory Health Partners

"This is a five-star book. If I could give it more stars I would. I can't say enough to encourage everyone to read these amazing words! I must say I have never read anything like it.

I couldn't wait to read each day the things I would have never asked myself about God or questioned God about; the way I pray, things I have never thought to ask God for or about.

Each page teaches something, and I love the question-and-answer part in the companion journal pages. They open your eyes to see exactly what we should be asking ourselves.

As you read deeper into this teaching, you experience God more intimately. Learning to hear Him speak to you is encouraging and keeps you wanting to read more.

I'm so blessed to have read these words. I can't explain my true feelings about this book the Holy Spirit guided Matcine Pepper to write. Without it, I would have never learned what I have been taught through this devotional and journal.

Thank you, Holy Spirit and Matcine. God speaks to me in many ways now. I have become a different person after reading the insight that flows out of these words. God truly loves us and wants us to know who He is. This book will help you to truly know Him."

—*Trish Wilson*

INSTRUCTIONS FOR THE READER

This is the companion journal for the devotional book, with the same title. Do You Truly Know Him? Or Just Know About Him? Originally I had the two books written as one Devotional/ Journal. But, as I was pondering one day, I felt a nudge from Holy Spirit to separate the two. With the main reason being, there are some people who do not like or have any interest in working in any type of journal. So, they would likely not buy the devotional if they were together in one book. Therefore, they would not be able to receive the benefit of the devotional alone.

Since the writings in both books were inspired by Holy Spirit, it would be better to have the books as two separate books that could be used side by side for those who are interested in having the benefits of both books.

As you read the devotional and hear what Holy Spirit is speaking to your heart, once you finish the daily reading, if you have the companion journal, find the matching journal worksheet with the same title. They are all in the same order, so you should be able to determine easily enough which pages they are on based on the Table of Contents.

The journal pages are broken down into three sections:
1. Highlights - Uses bullet-points to highlight what the devotional pages cover.
2. Reflections - Asks pertinent questions to help you to think about where you are in your spiritual journey.
3. Apply it to Your Life - Gives you insight and instructions on ways you can grow in your walk spiritually, as well as giving scripture references that pertain to the title of the entry for that day.

As you endeavor to read the devotional and work the journal pages daily, please don't feel rushed to get through a day if you are needing more time to work out your thoughts or feelings. There is nothing that says you absolutely have to complete this book in 32 days. It would be better for you to take your time and slowly process your responses through prayer and searching the scriptures than rushing through and missing something you need to see.

This should be a good experience for all who read the book and work the journal; to help you grow spiritually and to help you overcome things that have held you back from growing.

There is an additional blank page after each journal page in case you need extra space to answer questions from that days entry. Please understand, God already knows the things in your heart, and sometimes writing your feelings and thoughts helps you to express them to Him. There may be times you feel at a loss for words to pray out loud. Often-times this is the case for me. It seems my thoughts (or many times Gods thoughts) flow more freely when I am writing.

I pray "that the God of our Lord Jesus Christ, the Father of glory, may give to you the spirit of wisdom and revelation in the knowledge of Him, the eyes of your understanding being enlightened; that you may know what is the hope of His calling, what are the riches of the glory of His inheritance in the saints, and what is the exceeding greatness of His power toward us who believe, according to the working of His mighty power" (Ephesians 1:17-19)

In the beginning...

A Man's Heart Plans His Way

Highlights

- Trust God through tests and trials.
- We overcome the enemy's power as we testify of God's faithfulness to carry us through the trials we face.
- Trials often reveal our need for Jesus.

Reflections

Think back on a specific time in your life when you were going through something really difficult. Did you go through this battle alone, or did you call on the name of Jesus to help you through? _____
_____
_____

If you called on Jesus or not, what was the outcome of the trial?_____
_____
_____

If you did call on Jesus, did you testify of His faithfulness to others about it?_____
_____
_____

We can't change the past, but we can learn from it. What's one thing you will do differently in the future when you go through something else difficult? _____
_____
_____

Apply it to Your Life

Acknowledge your need for help and guidance and trust Jesus, through Holy Spirit, to help you in the tests and trials you face.

"Trust in the Lord with all your heart, and lean not on your own understanding; In all your ways acknowledge Him, and He shall direct your paths."

Proverbs 3:5-6

Notes

Be As Wise As A Serpent

Highlights

- We're in a spiritual battle.
- When we're weak in faith, the enemy knows.
- When we're strong in faith, the enemy knows.
- We must be bold as a Lion by taking our spiritual authority.
- We must know the Word of God to be as wise as serpents.

Reflections

As you face trials or battles in life, do you know how to stand on the Word of God, or does the enemy devour you and cause you to feel powerless and hopeless?_____

_____

_____

Is your faith weak or strong? If weak, what is one thing you will do to change it? _____

_____

_____

_____

Apply it to Your Life

Remember, to have strong faith, you need to read the Word of God regularly. If you only read the Word occasionally, you will be weak in faith, just as you would be weak in your body if you only eat occasionally. The Word nourishes our spirits, just as food should nourish our bodies.

"Behold, I send you out as sheep in the midst of wolves. Therefore, be wise as serpents and harmless as doves."
Matthew 10:16

Notes

Who Am I That You Are Mindful Of Me

Highlights

- The Creator of the Universe, not only created the Universe, but He created you and me. We are only a vapor in the vastness of His beautiful Creation.
- According to His design, we are not insignificant. But, compared to Him, we are only filthy rags.
- We were formed with intricate detail, yet unique in every way, designed with God's DNA in us.
- We are either made male or female in His image. He knew exactly what color our eyes, skin, and hair color would be, how short or tall we would be, and even knew how many hairs would be on our heads.
- We were all created and born with a specific purpose for such a time as this.
- We are a spirit, we have a soul, and we live in a body. Our spirits are what connects us with God, our souls are our mind, will, and emotions. Our bodies contain these two opposing forces within them. The soul is the fleshly realm we live in that is always longing to satisfy the desires of the flesh, and is responsible for keeping us in sin. Also known as our carnal nature.
- Because we were born in sin doesn't mean we have to die in sin. It is truly our choice to live eternally or to die eternally.
- In Christ, when we cease living in this body and our spirits leave, we will be eternally joined with The Father, God, and The Son, Jesus, in Heaven. We will walk on the streets of gold, never remembering our former life here on earth. Isaiah 65:17
- Apart from Christ, when our body breathes its last breath, our spirits will leave and be sent into the abyss to spend all eternity with satan; the one who deceived all who join him. They will never be satisfied and will be tormented throughout eternity, with weeping and gnashing of teeth. (Matthew 25:1-46)

Reflections

Have you ever considered, that although you had earthly parents whom God used as a means of your birth, you were intended to be here before the earth's foundations were formed? _____
_____
_____

How does it make you feel to know God thought specifically of you and created you uniquely for such a time as this? _____
_____
_____

Have you ever believed the lie that God doesn't love you or care anything about what happens to you? _____
_____
_____

Do you still believe this lie? _____
_____
_____

If so, why? _____
_____
_____

Do you know what God's plan and purpose for your life is? _____
_____
_____

If yes, what do you feel He's called you to do?_____
_____
_____

What are some things you feel He has gifted you to do? _____
_____
_____

Often, if not always, the special gifts and talents God has given us, are part of our calling. So, if you're good at art, you might look into trying your hand at prophetic art. If singing, maybe you could look into being on a worship team in church, or if musically gifted, maybe singing and worshiping with instruments. Pray for His direction and plan. Many are encouragers and can help to encourage others, while others have a gift to teach and help others to understand things better. Maybe writing is your gift. There are many other giftings He can give. These are just a few ideas to get your thoughts going.

Do you long to live righteous and holy, but struggle with sin and fear you may not be found worthy of going to heaven when you die?_____
_____
_____

Apply it to Your Life

Press into God and be transparent before Him as you tell Him what you're struggling with. Ask Him to take the desire to do these things away. Renounce this sin and tell it you are no longer going to let it have power over you, because "greater is He who is in you than he who is in the world." Stay humble before God and He will honor your heart's cry, and help you to fully overcome the things that the enemy has used to keep you in bondage.

Often, in order to walk in full freedom, it is a process. You must keep pressing into Him and you will grow stronger each day as you look to God for your strength and help. Don't let condemnation from the enemy cause you to pull away from God. He will use shame or anything else to cause you to turn away from God. Remember, he hates losing someone who used to live for him and has all sorts of tricks up his sleeve to keep you from fulfilling God's plan for your life.

"Therefore if the Son makes you free, you shall be free indeed."

John 8:36

"Keep yourselves in the love of God, looking for the mercy of our Lord Jesus Christ unto eternal life."

Jude 1:21

"For I know the thoughts that I think toward you says the Lord, thoughts of peace and not of evil, to give you a future and a hope. Then you will call upon Me and go and pray to Me, and I will listen to you. And you will seek Me and find Me, when you search for Me with all of your heart. I will be found by you, says the Lord, and I will bring you back from your captivity;"

Jeremiah 29:11-14a

"For behold, I create new heavens and a new earth; And the former shall not be remembered or come to mind."

Isaiah 65:17

Notes

Many Are The Afflictions Of The Righteous

Highlights

- We live in a fallen world therefore we will all suffer in our lives.
- With Christ, we don't suffer as those with no hope.
- Rejection is a spirit that enters us; bringing lies meant to destroy us.
- The power of the blood of Jesus is greater than any lie or deception of the enemy.
- Humility and surrender will help you to truly know Him and no longer just know about Him.
- Death, hell, and the grave were defeated by Jesus.

Reflections

Are there things you've struggled with throughout your life that you don't seem to be able to get past?_____

_____

_____

Physical, emotional, and mental pain can often be strongholds from generational curses. Many types of strongholds can keep us from walking in the freedom of Christ. A few examples are spirits of rejection, anger, unforgiveness, hopelessness, hate, perversion, lust, and so many more. They're all rooted in lies from the enemy of your soul.

If these are things you've battled with, make a list of all that you know of. Ask the Holy Spirit to show you anything you may not be aware of. Whatever He shows you, repent and renounce coming into agreement with the lies. Ask Him to set you free of these strongholds.

_____

_____

_____

_____

_____

_____

Apply it to Your Life

As you learn who you are in Christ and who He is in you, you will learn to walk in your spiritual authority. The devil will then be forced to let go of his grip on you.

"Who the Son Makes free, is free indeed."

John 8:36

Notes

My Testimony of Hope Restored

Highlights

- Turn to God when life offers no hope. He is the God of hope.
- We can never get so far down that God can't reach us.
- When we call out to Him, He will reach out to us.
- When our hope is restored there is power in our testimonies to help set others free.
- Always be willing to testify of the grace and the goodness of God.

Reflections

Has there ever been a time in your life when you felt so hopeless you wanted to give up?_____
_____
_____

Are you still in that place, or did your situation turn around? _____
_____
_____

If you've come out of it, what was the turning point for you?_____
_____
_____

Do you believe God turned things around for you? If so, have you testified of how God brought you through this difficult time? Maybe you can write out your testimony and have it available to share with others if God opens the door to make it happen. It's always good to be prepared if you are willing to be used by God to help others.

_____
_____
_____
_____
_____
_____
_____
_____
_____
_____
_____
_____

Apply it to Your Life

If you are still struggling, call on the name of Jesus. Ask Him to deliver you from this dark place and to have mercy on you. Surrender your life to Him through repentance. This will shut any opened doors to the enemy, so that you can walk in God's peace. Ask Him to set you free from the darkness and help you to walk in His freedom and light. Ask Him to expose all of the lies of the enemy and to help you stand in your authority as a child of God. Read His Word so that you know how to not only walk in freedom but to also help others do the same. Testify of His delivering power to all who will listen. Walk in your freedom and know you are loved.

"Therefore if the Son makes you free, you shall be free indeed."

John 8:36

"Hope deferred makes the heart sick, But when the desire comes, it is a tree of life."

Proverbs 13:12

"And they overcame him by the blood of the lamb and the word of their testimony, and they did not love their lives to the death."

Revelation 12:11

Notes

Posture Your Heart

Highlights

- Know the Word of God through reading it, and you will recognize His voice when He speaks.
- God will speak truth to you even if it is difficult to hear because He loves you.
- God chastens those He loves.
- Follow His commands; obey, and He will protect you from "the stranger," satan.
- You can only walk with Him if you truly know Him.
- You cannot fool God.

Reflections

Can you hear the voice of God when He speaks? _____
_____
_____

What are some of the ways He speaks to you most often? In a still small voice (as a thought or an idea)? Through scripture? Someone else speaking? In your writing? Any other way?_____
_____
_____

Are you quick to repent when you sin or do anything that would grieve Him? _____
_____
_____

    If you do slip up and sin and you are not quick to repent, it's a good thing to start doing so. Doing this will keep the slate clean, and you will not be as likely to keep messing up with the things that used to be commonplace with you. Ask the Holy Spirit to help prompt you so that you don't continue falling into the same habits of sin. Also, repenting will keep your heart tender and not allow pride or hardness to form within you. Staying humble before God will keep you close to God. He knows when we mess up, so when we are open and transparent before Him, He will cleanse us once again and cancel out that sin as if it never happened.

Do you seek Him with all of your heart, or do you seek Him with your heart at all? _____
_____
_____
_____
_____
_____
_____

Apply it to Your Life

God wants to reveal things to you that will strengthen you and protect you from the schemes of the enemy. He can only do this as you surrender your will to His. You will then discover His purpose for your life as you trust Him and stop trying to control things you can't control. If you fight against God (this is pride), you're giving the devil permission to devour you. If you work with God (this is humility), then His hand of protection will be upon you to stop the enemy from destroying your life.

"Seek the Lord while He may be found, Call upon Him while He is near."

Isaiah 55:6

"You shall love the Lord your God with all of your heart, with all your soul, and with all your strength."

Deuteronomy 6:5

"But He gives more grace. Therefore He says: "God resists the proud, But gives grace to the humble."

John 4:6

Notes

Reveal Anything In My Heart That Is Not Of You

Highlights

* God hears us when we pray.
* He loves a heart that is humble and willing to ask Him to expose things in us that we need His help with.
* He loves it when we are transparent, not trying to hide anything.
* He will give us the boldness to share the hope in us with others as we ask Him to.
* He loves when we give Him thanksgiving and praise as we pray.
* He is quick to forgive when we repent.

Reflections

Have you ever asked God to reveal anything in your heart that might be keeping you separated from Him or from hearing His voice? _____
_____
_____

If you do ask and He shows you something, do you repent and ask Him to forgive you and to cleanse you again?
_____
_____
_____

Do you try to hide anything in prayer? _____
_____
_____

Apply it to Your Life

God is all-seeing and all-knowing. There is nothing you can hide from Him, and when we try, He knows. He is quick to forgive and is waiting to take the burdens off of you! Don't let fear, worry, doubt, shame, rejection, anger, unforgiveness, hate, or anything keep you bound. Confess your struggles and lay them on the altar (You do this symbolically as you are praying by telling Him you are surrendering whatever it may be to Him). Let Jesus remove the burdens of these things so you can be free. Let the blood that Jesus shed on the cross have its full work in your life. Don't let what He did for you and me be wasted.

"The heart is deceitful above all things, And desperately wicked; Who can know it?"

Jeremiah 17:9

"Your word I have hidden in my heart, that I might not sin against You."

Psalms 119:11

Notes

Saved From My Sin

Highlights

- When Jesus sets us free, He will use us to help set others free.
- There is no sin so great that God won't forgive you for it.
- No matter how big or small sin might seem, it's still sin, and you can be forgiven.

Reflections

Have you been saved and forgiven from your sin? _____

_____

_____

If saved, did peace fill your heart when you asked Jesus into your life to cleanse you? _____
Maybe you experienced other emotions. Do you recall how you felt when you invited Jesus into your life?_____

_____

_____

Have you fallen for the lie that the sins you've committed are too horrible for Him to forgive? If so, sincerely give Him a try, and see if He doesn't make a difference in your life. What have you got to lose? Everything. What have you got to gain? Everything! _____

_____

_____

Apply it to Your Life

Just as the poem states, God loves us and saves us from all of our sin, no matter how big or small. The blood that Jesus shed as he hung on the cross was poured out to cleanse us and make us whole. He died so that we could be reunited back to the Father, as Jesus took our sin upon Himself and set us free from the power of sin and death.

"But God demonstrates His own love toward us, in that while we were still sinners, Christ died for us."

Romans 5:8

"There is therefore now no condemnation to those who are in Christ Jesus, who do not walk according to the flesh, but according to the Spirit."

Romans 8:1

Notes

Submit To God

Highlights

- When we submit and surrender to God, the enemy has to go through Him to get to us.
- If you are not walking in victory, you might not be truly submitted to God.
- If you're trying to walk holy in your efforts, this is dead works and will leave you feeling empty and frustrated.
- Spiritual mentors are valuable, providing guidance to help you have a strong foundation in your faith.
- You must first have faith in God to submit to Him.
- God is not a pawn who can be controlled or manipulated. He is Righteous and Holy.

Reflections

Is there a specific time in your life when you felt overwhelmed and overcome by the battle you were facing? How was your relationship with God at that time?_____

_____

_____

Were you attempting in your effort to resolve this battle, or was your heart submitted to Him, trusting He would walk you through your struggle?_____

_____

_____

What was the outcome after this situation passed?_____

_____

_____

What will you do differently in the next battle?_____

_____

_____

Apply it to Your Life

Resisting the devil will not keep us from facing struggles or trials; we live in a fallen world. As we give our lives to God (submit to Him), He will give us the wisdom and strength we need to overcome the battle and have victory. When we are submitted to God, we can walk in our authority as children of God, and the devil will no longer be able to torment us. Satan knows when we know our authority in Christ. We command him to leave, in the name of Jesus!

"Therefore submit to God. Resist the devil and he will flee from you."

James 4:7

We can't submit to Christ if we don't fully surrender to Him. Surrendering is letting go of our right to live our lives as we please, and giving Him the right to live through us. We can then submit to His authority, which gives us the right to resist the devil. Then, because we are walking in God's perfect order, the devil has no choice but to flee and quit tormenting our lives. He must obey God's Word. He knows it better than anyone but God Himself. God is faithful to His Word and promises, and will never renege on anything He says He will do.

"But without faith it is impossible to please Him, for he who comes to God must believe that He is, and that He is a rewarder of those who diligently seek Him."

Hebrews 11:6

"God is not a man that he should lie, Nor a son of man, that He should repent. Has He said, and will He not do? Or has He spoken, and will He not make it good?"

Numbers 23:19

Notes

Thank You For Making A Way Of Escape

Highlights

- God always makes a way of escape from temptations if we are seeking Him in our lives.
- If we are born again, seeking God's will for our lives, the Holy Spirit is in us to help us resist temptations.
- We no longer have to depend on our conscience to guide us.
- Just because He makes a way of escape doesn't mean we will always choose His way.
- Rebellion will hinder us from walking in the blessings of God.
- We are set apart for His glory. The ultimate Way of Escape He gave us was through the blood of Jesus.

Reflections

Are you tempted by sin often? Do you give in to the temptations, or do you call on Jesus to help you to resist the temptations? _____
_____
_____

If you do fall short and sin, are you quick to repent and ask Holy Spirit to help by taking the desire to sin away? Or do you just go on as if nothing ever happened, hoping God will not see it as a big deal? _____
_____
_____

Is your heart hard and bound because of pain from your past? Do you find it hard to forgive and let go of this un-forgiveness and resentment? _____
_____
_____

Apply it to Your Life

There are no gray areas with God. It's either black or white. Sin is sin and it will condemn you or convict you. Satan will condemn you causing you to feel guilt or shame, and make you want to hide. God will convict you, causing you to want to repent and be made clean and whole once again. He is quick to forgive those who are quick to repent.

If you answered yes to the last question, this is sin and it will keep you from walking in God's forgiveness. Release the pain to Jesus. Repent and receive God's forgiveness. Choose to forgive so that YOU are no longer held captive by the enemy in the snare he set for you. This unforgiveness does not affect the other party, but only you, even if it's against yourself. Let it go, and be free my friend. Bitterness will only serve to torment you. Haven't you been tormented long enough now?

God has made a way of escape from anything the enemy will use to cause us to fall away from His grace and blessings. Humble yourself and let your pride go; it will be your downfall if you don't. Be free and filled with His joy and peace.

"Then when desire has conceived, it gives birth to sin; and sin, when it is full-grown, brings forth death."

James 1:15

(Ways of Escape)

"For if you forgive men their trespasses, your heavenly Father will also forgive you."

Matthew 6:14

"Teach me Your way, O Lord, And lead me in a smooth path, because of my enemies."

Psalms 27:11

"Let him know that he who turns a sinner from the error of his way will save a soul from death and cover a multitude of sins."

James 5:20

Notes

Your Birth Gave Me Life And Purpose

Highlights

- We were all created in many ways alike, yet in many more ways different.
- We were created in God's image.
- We were born into sin due to rebellion and pride.
- Jesus came to set us free from the power of sin over our lives.
- We can walk in blessings or curses; the choice is ours.
- We were born with purpose. In Jesus, we will fulfill our purpose. Apart from Him, we will die in our sin.

Reflections

Do you know God created you before He formed the earth? He knew your name, when you would be born, when you would die, how many hairs are on your head, and every intricate detail about you. Have you ever believed you were of such value that the Creator of the Universe cares about everything that concerns you? If not, how come?

_____

_____

_____

Do you understand that although you were born with many traits and characteristics of your earthly parents, you also have the DNA of your Heavenly Father?_____

_____

_____

Did you know He has placed special gifts and talents in you to enable you to fulfill your purpose? _____

_____

_____

Have you discovered some of your giftings and how He intends to use them to bring the lost into their place in the kingdom? _____

_____

_____

Make a list of anything you feel God has imparted to you to help you walk in your purpose. It could be ministry in some capacity, serving others, singing, art, writing, the gift of compassion, the financial stability to help support others in need, and many other ways to help shine His light for others to see and to come to Him:

_____

_____

_____

_____

Apply it to Your Life

He will show you as you seek Him to know what your giftings and talents are. Then ask Him to help you to develop them if you haven't already. He will shine brightly through you as you avail yourself of Him.

"Having then gifts differing according to the grace that is given to us, let us use them: if prophecy, let us prophesy in proportion to our faith; or ministry, let us use it in our ministering; he who teaches, in teaching; he who exhorts, in exhortation; he who gives, with liberality; he who leads, with diligence; he who shows mercy, with cheerfulness."

Romans 12:6-8

"And these signs will follow those who believe: In my name they will cast out demons; they will speak with new tongues; they will take up serpents; and if they drink anything deadly, it will by no means hurt them; they will lay hands on the sick and they will recover."

Mark 16:17-18

Notes

The Journey To Wholeness

A New Life Has Begun

Highlights

- Without a loving Savior, our lives are hopeless and empty with no true purpose.
- God can reveal our need for Jesus in many ways. Even in a dream, He can reveal our eternal destination is not secure if we don't turn to Him for salvation.
- When Jesus comes into our lives, we have a life-changing transformation.
- Becoming a Christian is more than saying a sinner's prayer. It's not what you say with your mouth; it's what you believe in your heart.
- We must be fully submerged in Him. Not half in and half out.
- As we surrender to Him, we begin to discover who we are in Him and who He is in us.

Reflections

Have you wondered what life is really about? Have you asked what is my purpose? Why was I born? Have you gotten any answers to these questions? If so, what do you believe they are? _____

_____

_____

If you already know Jesus, what are some of the ways He's revealed Himself to you? Maybe through a pastor or teacher? A friend or stranger? A family member? In a dream, vision, or any other way He can show up for us to find Him? _____

_____

_____

If you don't know Him, have you had any of the above experiences and felt hesitant to respond because you didn't feel ready to pay the price, thinking you would have to give up too much to surrender it all? Maybe there is another reason. Try to explain if you can. _____

_____

_____

If you prayed a "sinner's prayer," did you pray it with a heart broken over your sin and truly desire to change? _____ Was there a real transformation that was obvious to you and others? _____ If so, what were some of the things that changed?_____

_____

_____

If you answered yes to the above question, Has God revealed or begun to reveal your true purpose for being born? Make a list of things He has revealed to you about the ways He wants to use you to pour His love out on others.

_____

_____

_____

Apply it to Your Life

We are all created and born with a purpose, but without Christ revealing our purpose to us, we will never realize our reason for being born. We will never reach our intended destiny without Christ in our lives. Fear often keeps people from receiving Jesus as their Savior. They believe the lie that they will have to give up too much and that the life of a Christian is boring. This could not be further from the truth. You will never give up more than you will gain, and often the things you give up become no longer of interest to you. It's a supernatural thing when Christ transforms us. Something almost impossible to explain. You just don't have the desire to continue to live the way you have been living. Your heart desires have been changed.

You will gain love, joy, peace, patience, kindness, goodness, and faithfulness. You will be filled with life and a desire to share that hope for the life you've been given to others. You will no longer be filled with hopelessness, depression, and despair. You will learn who you are in Christ and learn to walk in your authority over the demonic realm that has robbed so much from you all of your life.

If the enemy can keep you from making the greatest decision of your life, he wins - you lose! If you call on the name of Jesus, and learn who you are in Christ, and who Christ is in you; if you learn to walk in your spiritual authority and no longer tolerate the devil dangling you around like a puppet on a string, then you win and he loses! He is already defeated and his time for ruling others is about to come to an end. However, when we realize who we are in Christ, it comes to an end in our lives much sooner.

"Therefore, laying aside all malice, all deceit, hypocrisy, envy, and all evil speaking, as newborn babes, desire the pure milk of the word, that you may grow thereby, if indeed you have tasted that the Lord is gracious."

I Peter 2:1-3

"But you are a chosen generation, a royal priesthood, a holy nation, His own special people, that you may proclaim the praises of Him who called you out of darkness into His marvelous light; who once were not a people but are now the people of God, who had not obtained mercy but now have obtained mercy."

I Peter 2:9-10

"Oh, taste and see that the Lord is good; Blessed is the man who trusts in Him!"

Psalms 34:8

Notes

A Prayer To Abide In God

Highlights

- There is no secret formula to abide in God. Just trust!
- Mentors can often help you learn to walk in trust, as they are used to minister His love and deliverance to you.
- Often with pain and trauma in our lives, having an intimate relationship with anyone, including God, is difficult.
- When God sets us free and we learn to abide in Him, He will use us to help others to overcome and be set free.
- When we abide in God, it slams the door shut for the enemy to continue the cycle of torment in our lives.

Reflections

If you have asked Jesus to be the Lord and Savior of your life, are you finding it easy or difficult to feel connected with Him? _____

_____

_____

If difficult, do you see that you might have trust issues hindering you?_____

Were you abused in any way when you were young, or did you suffer some painful trauma that is keeping you from being able to trust?_____

If you are unaware of any abuse, neglect, or trauma, ask God to reveal anything you may have forgotten. If He shows you anything, write it down. _____

_____

_____

Apply it to Your Life

Ask Him to walk you through the forgiveness process so He can set you free. Either way, whether you remember or you don't, if you are holding unforgiveness towards anyone, then you need to forgive. Forgiveness is the first step to your healing process after salvation. The Word of God says that if we don't forgive others their sins, neither will He forgive us. Unforgiveness towards others is a sin in God's eyes. Sin cannot be in the presence of a Holy God. So, if you are feeling disconnected from God, ask Him to forgive you for having unforgiveness in your heart, and choose to forgive anyone in your life you are holding unforgiveness towards. Release them and be set free! (This is not necessarily the only reason to feel disconnected from God, but is often the greatest hindrance).

If someone committed a sin against you, they will be held accountable to God. If they die in their sin without repentance, they will be judged according to their sin. We will all stand before Him one day, either guilty–charged with our sin, or innocent–cleansed by the blood of Jesus and free of guilt. Whole and complete in Him!

Ask Him to send you a mentor! A godly man for men or woman for women is always best so that no one is easily tempted by satan. You will want someone who walks closely with God, and who has a heart to minister to others who are finding it difficult getting established in their walk with the Lord. Mentors don't usually classify themselves as such; it's through their lifestyle and strength in their walk with God that you will recognize them. Others may also recommend someone to you, someone with a godly character to help you with things you need help with.

There are professional mentors and life coaches who charge for their services. Depending on your needs, some of you may choose to go this route, but if you do, be wise and be sure to do your due diligence in searching for someone and vetting them before paying for any services. But for most, God will likely bring a seasoned Christian into your life to help mentor/disciple you as He did for me. This will enable you to be used as a vessel to bring Glory to the One who laid His life down to save your soul and set you free.

"For if you forgive men their trespasses (sin), your heavenly Father will also forgive you. But if you do not forgive men their trespasses, neither will your Father forgive your trespasses."

Matthew 6:14-15

"Heal the sick, cleanse the lepers, raise the dead, cast out demons. Freely you have received, freely give."

Matthew 10:8

"Abide in Me, and I in you. As the branch cannot bear fruit of itself, unless it abides in the vine, neither can you, unless you abide in Me."

John 15:4

Notes

Awaken You Who Slumber

Highlights

- The One who created us will soon return. The time is drawing near. Time to prepare is running out.
- Do you truly know Him or just know about Him? Many will be eternally separated from Him if they only know about Him.
- We were created to be one with Him; this was completed when Jesus died on the cross. Because He gave us free will, it's up to us to decide if we will know Him or not.
- We were created with a void that only He can fill. Without Him, we will always be empty and wanting.
- He will return in the twinkling of an eye. Waiting till it's too late to call on Him will cause us to be cast into outer darkness; we will be forever tormented and our thirst will never be quenched.
- If we turn our backs on Him, He will turn His on us. Today is the day of salvation.

Reflections

Have you had a salvation experience where there is beyond a shadow of doubt you had a heart-transforming experience? _____
Explain how you felt afterward, anywhere from a day to several weeks later._____
_____
_____

If you truly did not change after this experience, what motivated you to respond to the call for salvation? Were you moved by fear of going to hell? Did you respond because your friends did, and you didn't want to be made fun of or feel condemned by them? Was there another reason? _____
_____
_____

Apply it to Your Life

If your reason for responding was motivated out of fear (as mentioned above), and not because of the fear of the Lord, or if you felt condemned, then your heart was not responding for the right reason. If you were not convicted in your heart that you are a sinner in need of a Savior, then you were responding for the wrong reason. God knows our hearts and He cannot be fooled. There is no salvation without a true heart of repentance—a heart sorry for sinning against God, wanting to be changed to live a life that is holy and pleasing to Him..

Once born again, seek to walk closely to God through reading His Word, praying daily and often. Learn about Him by being committed to truly knowing Him. Your life will never be the same. He will use you in ways you never imagined He would, showing you great and mighty things. You will no longer be tormented by the enemy; God will use you as a vessel against the enemy, causing you to stand in your authority as His child.

"Jesus said to him, "I am the way, the truth, and the life. No one comes to the Father except through Me."

John 14:6

"And if I go and prepare a place for you, I will come again and receive you to Myself; that where I am, there you may be also."

John 14:3

"Let us be glad and rejoice and give Him glory, for the marriage of the Lamb has come, and His wife has made herself ready."

Revelation 19:7

"Watch therefore, for you know neither the day nor the hour in which the Son of Man is coming."

Matthew 25:13

"For God so loved the world that He gave His only begotten Son. That whosoever believes in Him shall not perish, but have eternal life. For God did not send His Son into the world to condemn the world, but that the world through Him might be saved."

John 3:16-17

Notes

Don't Conform, Be Transformed

Highlights

- To no longer be conformed to this world, we must be transformed—first by the power of Christ in us, and second, by renewing our minds through reading the Word of God.
- When (not if) the storms come, how we navigate through them will determine if they toss us back and forth like the waves of the sea, or if we have peace in the midst of the storms.
- We become like what we focus on. Our thoughts and lives will reflect what has our attention. Either good or bad will spill out of us, depending on our focus.
- We must renew our minds by changing our focus from the things of this world to the Word of His Truth.
- As we seek God, He will be found. This is the key to truly knowing Him. As we come to truly know Him, we become more like Him, and our lives are transformed more into His image.
- Being transformed reveals who you are in Christ. We discover our spiritual authority and are no longer powerless when the enemy comes to torment us. We stand in our place of authority and now command satan to flee!

Reflections

Do you often feel hopeless or powerless when you are challenged with things too difficult to face? _____
_____
_____

What are some of those challenges? Attacks on your body (health) or your mind? Maybe against your family? Things happening in your home? These are just a few of the many possibilities to help you think._____
_____
_____

What are your feelings or responses when something challenging arises? Fear, dread, anxiety, hopelessness?
_____
_____
_____

If you're a follower of Christ (a Christian), do you daily spend time reading the Word and prayerfully asking Holy Spirit to enlighten you to what He is speaking to you when you read it? _____
_____
_____

Do you seek wisdom and insight about specific challenges you are facing as you read, and not just reading for the sake of saying you read the Bible daily? _____
_____
_____

Are you more focused on the news and the things happening in the world, and less focused on learning how to walk in faith and truth? _____

_____

_____

Apply it to Your Life

The Word is instrumental in helping us when we face challenges….

There is power in the Word of God. My niece just expressed, "It is alive and breathing." It has the power to bring life to anyone who is truly hungry for the knowledge of His truth to come alive in them. It is the only life-giving, inspired Word of God with the power to redeem, restore, heal, deliver, and transform us all.

You can read all of the self-help books, go to all of the motivational seminars, hire the best life coaches, and try every religious group there is or ever was, but even with the very best the world has to offer, nothing can give you the transforming peace, hope, love, joy, or life that the Word of God alone can give. Not only does it offer all of these earthly blessings, but through the Word, we are taught how to have a personal relationship with Jesus Christ.

Through this relationship with Jesus, as we've made Him our Lord and Savior, we are also assured eternal life. We, through truly getting to know Him, are promised we will spend eternity with Jesus and the Father. We will walk on streets of gold, spending time worshiping our Creator and Heavenly Father with all the other Saints who have gone to join Him before and after us.

Life will always present challenges to us since we live in a fallen world, but renewing our minds and becoming transformed is the key to living a victorious life and a life with purpose.

"For I know the thoughts that I think toward you, says the Lord, thoughts of peace and not of evil, to give you a future and a hope."

Jeremiah 29:11

"And you will seek Me and find Me, when you search for Me with all your heart."

Jeremiah 29:13

"And do not be conformed to this world, but be transformed by the renewing of your mind, that you may prove what is that good and acceptable and perfect will of God."

Romans 12:2

"But the Helper, the Holy Spirit, whom the Father will send in My name, He will teach you all things, and bring to your remembrance all things that I said to you."

John 14:26

"And you shall know the truth, and the truth shall make you free."

John 8:32

Notes

Dwell And Abide

Highlights

- We confide in Him in the "secret place" (our special place of prayer) and set aside time to come to Him in prayer.
- He will protect and cover us in the shadow of His wings.
- His Word is truth, our shield, and will protect us when we must fight spiritual battles.
- No arrow by day, or terror at night, or anything else will cause us harm or fear. His Word will show us the way!
- A thousand may fall at your side, ten thousand at your right hand, but its foundation is sinking sand.
- The angels will bear you up, lest you dash your foot upon a stone.
- He will satisfy you with a long life as you choose to truly know Him.
- Dwell and abide in the Lord Most High, and He will deliver you. He has much for you to do!

Reflections

When you're praying, do you understand that nothing is off-limits with God? He is omniscient, all-knowing. There is nothing we can hide from Him, and it's His desire that we come openly to Him in prayer. No pretending, no fear, no doubt or unbelief that He will receive you with open arms. He knows each of us, as He created us before the foundations of the earth. He knows our thoughts and even knows if we are walking in pride, or if our heart is sincere before Him. So, when you are in prayer (the secret place), are you open with Him, or hesitant to be open?_____

What are some of the things you struggle with when you are talking to God (Father, Daddy, Papa)? _____
_____
_____

When we dedicate our time to learning His Word and growing in our understanding and knowledge of Who He is in us and who we are in Him, then when we are faced with battles in life, when the enemy is trying to discourage us or to trip us up, we can fight our battles with His Word and promises.

Do you know how to stand in the authority of God's Word when you're facing a challenge and you know the enemy is working against you?_____
_____
_____

Do you have a set time for daily Bible reading (either the Book or an App)? _____

Do you know your authority in Christ and how to use it?_____ If yes, what are some of the ways you've used the power of God's Word against the enemy? _____
_____

Apply it to Your Life

Even if you are a new believer, learn as much as you can from reading the Word. Memorizing scripture is good, but it's not completely necessary to memorize it, as Holy Spirit will bring to your remembrance what you need when you need it. At times you might have to cry out, "Help Me, Jesus." He is a very present help in times of trouble.

As you learn who God is, you become acquainted with Him, and as you do, you will be strengthened in your spirit, your soul, and your body. In our weakness, He is made strong. When we grow in Him, we are growing in our strength through Him, and more in our understanding of who we are in Him.

In most cases it's easier to include reading the Word as you are spending time in prayer. That way, you can also practice praying God's Word back to Him. He loves it when we stand on His Word and recall it to Him. His Word became flesh and dwelt (lived) among us. This means, because we are now walking in Christ, that He is alive in us and when we stand on His Word by speaking it, we are walking in His Spirit and Truth. Jesus, by the power of His Holy Spirit, is alive in us, and it's in Him we live, move, and have our being.

When we use the Word in battles we are dealing with, it becomes a weapon in our hands. It's like a two-edged sword, and speaking it against the enemy will send him running. He hates when a Child of God knows their authority. We remove his power from him and he can't get away from us quickly enough.

If we are not using the Word against the enemy because we are weak in our knowledge of the Word, he will use it against us. One example of this is in Matthew 4:1-11, after Jesus had been fasting for 40 days, and then satan came to tempt Him to worship him. Three times he attempted to cause Him to stumble by using God's Word against Him. Each time Jesus used the Word back against the devil by saying, "It is written." When we know what is written, we will not be easy targets for the enemy to destroy. "Greater is He who is in us than he who is in the world." When we dwell in Him, and He abides in us, we are a mighty fortress against the gates of hell and they will not prevail against us.

"God is our refuge and strength, A very present help in trouble."

Psalms 46:1

And He said to me, "My grace is sufficient for you, for My strength is made perfect in weakness." Therefore most gladly I will rather boast in my infirmities, that the power of Christ may rest upon me.

2 Corinthians 12:9

"And the Word became flesh and dwelt among us, and we beheld His glory, the glory as of the only begotten of the Father, full of grace and truth."

John 1:14

"For in Him we live and move and have our being, as also some of your own poets have said, 'For we are also His offspring.'"

Acts 17:28

"You are of God little children, and have overcome them, because He who is in you is greater than he who is in the world."

1 John 4:4

Notes

Illuminate All Darkness

Highlights

- God's light will illuminate all darkness so the darkness can't hide. It will be exposed and expelled through the light of His Word.
- Our lights shine brightly when we are more concerned with how God sees us than how others see us.
- Only in a deep relationship with God will He reveal His heart and plans to us. This is how to walk in the fullness of His grace and love.
- When He reveals anything in you that causes you to be separated from Him, be quick to repent and ask for forgiveness. Then turn from those things and seek Him with your whole heart.
- Being humbled and submitted to Him causes you to grow in your Christian walk.

Reflections

Do you feel there is darkness or something hindering you from walking in the full freedom of the Cross? Things you really can't explain? _____

Are your thoughts scattered and keeping you from being focused on one thing at a time? _____

_____

Do you feel unable to take your thoughts captive (Unable to maintain focus)? _____

Are you committed to spending time reading and studying the Word daily? _____

Apply it to Your Life

Many things are vying for our attention. When we finally come to the place of seeing our need for God to become first in our lives, the enemy knows he will lose his power over us. He knows our weaknesses and will do anything in his power to distract us and keep us from drawing closer to God.

These distractions can come in many ways. Thoughts of things you need to do suddenly, interruptions from others, pain in your body, thoughts about something you said to someone or something someone said to you, how someone hurt you; you get it! He is a master of distractions, and we must resist him and his distractions at all costs. We are to be single-minded, and not have a divided heart. Gods Word is the key to us being single-minded.

The enemy uses other tactics to keep us from reading the Word too! The greatest one is a spirit of slumber. Often you might suddenly feel overwhelmingly tired and can hardly keep your eyes open when reading scripture or listening to a sermon or a message from the Word. When you feel this begin to happen, take your spiritual authority, and tell that spirit to leave in Jesus' name. Say it with authority! That belongs to you as a child of God. When the enemy pushes himself on you, push back and command Him to GO, in Jesus' name!

"Your Word is a lamp to my feet and a light to my path."

Psalms 119:105

"Behold, I have given you the authority to trample on serpents and scorpions, and over all the power of the enemy, and nothing shall by any means hurt you."

Luke 10:19

Notes

In My Weakness You Are Made Strong

Highlights

- Apart from God, we are empty, helpless, and lacking in every area of our lives.
- God has a plan and a purpose for our lives.
- When we are separated from God in our hearts, we are not walking a surrendered life.
- Our will is self-seeking, leading to spiritual and eternal death.
- God's will is purposeful, and fulfilling, leading to spiritual and eternal life.
- As long as we are humble and seeking His will, we will walk the way He designed us to—Holy and pleasing to Him.

Reflections

If you've prayed to receive Jesus as your Lord and Savior, reflect on these things:

Do you feel empty and hopeless, or fulfilled and full of hope? _____

_____

_____

Do you know you have a purpose for being alive? If yes, what do you feel it is?_____

_____

_____

What are you doing to ensure you're growing in your relationship with Christ? _____

_____

_____

Are you testifying to others about what God has done in your life and of the hope you have in Christ? _____

_____

_____

Has your lifestyle changed? Are you less interested in doing things you used to do and more interested in learning about God and what His will and plans for your life are?_____

_____

What are some of the things you used to enjoy doing that are no longer of interest to you?_____

_____

_____

Have you been delivered or set free from any darkness or oppression such as anger; depression; a spirit of suicide; any drug, alcohol, or other addictions; porn or sexual perversions; cussing; gossiping; unforgiveness; spirit of rejection; mental illness; lying; or any other strongholds that have had you bound?_____

_____

_____

Apply it to Your Life

If you are still living in sin and are okay with it, then you need to really search your heart about your commitment to God and seek God's heart about how you're living.

If, however, you are battling with sin, this doesn't necessarily mean you are not saved, but it does mean you may still be bound in some areas and need to be set free. Seek God in prayer and confess that you need the Holy Spirit to help you. Being humble before God is always one of the main keys to your freedom. Ask Him to lead you to scriptures that will reveal what you need to know: 1. About who Christ is in you, 2. Who you are in Christ, 3. About the strongholds you're struggling with, 4. How to be set free from the strongholds of the enemy. Perhaps consider asking God to lead you to a church that has a deliverance ministry that can help you to be set free.

Often as you grow in your walk with Christ, these things will no longer have power over you. But, sometimes it takes a little while to walk in the full freedom of the cross. God will always complete what He begins, so don't get discouraged or lose hope. As long as you seek Him, you will grow in Him and your strength will be made stronger through Him. Part of your growth will include learning your spiritual authority over the realms of darkness. When you know who you are in Christ, demons will not bother you as they once did.

"And He said to me, "'My grace is sufficient for you, for My strength is made perfect in weakness."' Therefore most gladly I will rather boast in my infirmities, that the power of Christ may rest upon me. Therefore I take pleasure in infirmities, in reproaches, in needs, in persecutions, in distresses, for Christ's sake. For when I am weak, then I am strong."

2 Corinthians 12:9-10

"I have been crucified with Christ; it is no longer I who live, but Christ lives in me; and the life which I now live in the flesh I live by faith in the Son of God, who loved me and gave Himself for me."

Galatians 2:20

"There is therefore now no condemnation to those who are in Christ Jesus, who do not walk according to the flesh, but according to the Spirit."

Romans 8:1

Notes

Obedience Is Better Than Sacrifice

Highlights

- Obedience is better than sacrifice.
- There is almost always a sacrifice involved when God calls us to do something.
- When we are disobedient to what God wants us to do, we are showing a lack of trust in Him and His plans for our lives.
- We don't have to have statues in our lives to have idols. Anything in our life that we give more focus to or put more value on than God is an idol. It can be in any form—yes, even people, electronic devices, statues, hobbies, sports, jobs, and the list goes on.

Reflections

Do you find it difficult to submit to authority? (Submitting to authority shows your willingness to follow the directions of those in authority over you, especially God.) _____
_____
_____

Do you have a hard time trusting God or others?_____
_____
_____

If yes, do you know why? Has anyone betrayed your trust, causing you to have trust issues?_____
_____
_____

Do you have things that you are consumed or obsessed with? Things such as your phone, electronic devices, games, hobbies, children or someone you love, religious idols that you believe will bring you "good luck" or protect you from evil or bad things happening, or anything that you are placing your focus on or giving your time to above God is an idol in your life._____
_____
_____

Apply it to Your Life

If you are a born-again believer and have idols in your life, then the chances that you have an issue with obedience are pretty high. If you are obsessed with anything above God, and lacking in discipline, this indicates a lack of trust in God, and these things have become a form of escape from deeper issues that you're not willing to face.

Others may have betrayed your trust, but rest assured, God will never turn His back on you! He will never gossip about you, abuse you, neglect you, or abandon you. He is a friend who sticks closer than a brother and will help you to overcome the betrayal and hurt inflicted by others. He is faithful and true to His Word and His promises. He will bless you as you step out in obedience to the things He asks you to do. He is the only One who can bring hope and purpose to your life.

"Now by this we know that we know Him, if we keep His commandments."

1 John 2:3

Notes

The Lord Of The Ring

Highlights

- Sometimes we may find ourselves in situations where we want or need something, and are willing to go into debt or sacrifice paying a bill to get it.
- Even if our heart and motives for having the thing is right or seems right, we should always pray for God's will and His plan in the matter.
- As we place our trust in God for our desires, He will reveal His answer. Although it may not always be the answer you want, when it is, He will make a way where there seems to be no way.
- God's blessings are always greater than anything we could ask or think of.

Reflections

Can you remember a time when you desired something, but really couldn't afford it, yet were willing to (or maybe did) go into debt to have it? What was the outcome of this test of trusting God (if you were walking with Him)?

_____

_____

_____

Were you led to trust Him and wait? _____

If yes, when the answer came, was it exactly what you wanted or beyond what you thought about? _____

_____

_____

Have you shared your testimony of God's faithfulness with others? _____ If yes, great; Keep up the good work! If not, is there a reason you haven't shared? Did you not think it would encourage others if you shared with them? _____

_____

_____

Apply it to Your Life

Maybe you need the assurance of salvation and have never asked Him to be Lord of your life. This is the first and most important prayer you can offer up to God, and if it's the only prayer He ever answers for you, it would still be His greatest gift to you.

He is faithful and true and loves to bless His children. When you're walking with Him in full trust, His blessings will come into your life. He loves to bless His children.

"For the Lord God is a sun and a shield; The Lord will give grace and glory; No good thing will He withhold from those who walk uprightly. O Lord of hosts, Blessed is the man who trusts in You!"

Psalms 84:11-12

"Trust in the Lord with all of your heart, And lean not on your own understanding; In all your ways acknowledge Him, And He shall direct your paths."

Proverbs 3:5-6

"And they (we) overcame him (satan) by the blood of the Lamb (Jesus) and by the word of their testimony, and they did not love their lives to the death."

Revelation 12:11

"Delight yourself also in the Lord, And He shall give you the desires of your heart."

Psalms 37:4

Notes

Wait Upon The Lord

Highlights

- Wait upon the Lord in all that you do.
- He gave us his best when He sent us His Son.
- He has much for us to do.
- Just knowing about Him doesn't make us His.
- To know Him is to love Him.
- Only knowing about Him could make you fall.
- As you walk and talk with Him, you're learning to abide.
- Today is the day to call on His name.

Reflections

There are many ways we can wait upon the Lord. We might have a major decision to make and are unsure of how to proceed or how to decide what to do. Maybe we need to seek Him about things we need to personally change in our lives. Or, maybe we just need to wait and listen quietly for Him to speak something to our hearts. Can you name a specific reason you've waited on the Lord? What was the outcome of your waiting? _____

_____

_____

Are you aware that He has you here for a specific purpose? Do you know what He has specifically called you to do?_____

_____

_____

Have you been made aware of any special giftings or talents He's given you? If so, what are they? _____

_____

_____

Many know about Jesus but don't truly know Him. Knowing Him goes beyond saying a sinner's prayer. It requires spending quality time with Him in an intimate relationship—such as spending time learning about Him through daily reading His Word, spending time worshiping Him, and praying to Him. Do you know that you know Him?_____What are some of the things you do to help ensure that you know Him? _____

_____

_____

If you've never had a personal encounter with the Lord, today is the day of salvation. Have you already asked Him to become Lord of your life? _____ If yes, what are some of the changes you've experienced as proof that you've been transformed and He's working in your life? _____

_____

_____

Apply it to Your Life

If you've not asked Him to be Lord of your life, and you're ready to surrender your life to Him, to be set free from your sin and death (eternal death), ask Him to forgive you for your sin. Ask Him to wash and cleanse you and to make you whole. Confess that you believe Jesus was born of a virgin and died on the cross for your sins to be washed away, that He arose on the third day. He ascended to Heaven to sit at the right hand of God the Father and will return soon for His bride to be joined with Him. Now commit yourself to reading the Word to learn about Him and His plan for your life. Continually pray and seek His truth for your life. Draw close to Him, and He will draw close to you.

"Wait on the Lord; Be of good courage, and He shall strengthen your heart; Wait I say, on the Lord"
Psalms 27:14

"But those who wait on the Lord shall renew their strength; They shall mount up with wings like eagles, They shall run and not grow weary, They shall walk and not faint."
Isaiah 40:31

"The Lord is good to those who wait for Him, To the soul who seeks Him."
Lamentations 3:25

"Draw near to God and He will draw near to you. Cleanse your hands, you sinners; and purify your hearts, you double-minded."
James 4:8

Notes

Your Love Knows No Bounds

Highlights

- Although God knows everything about us, He still loves us.
- We usually have to get to the end of ourselves to see our emptiness and the need for God to rescue us.
- It's His Spirit wooing us with His unconditional (Agape) love that leads us to repentance.
- Apart from Him in our lives, we will never shine or offer any hope to others.
- He uses our circumstances and the hopelessness they sometimes bring, and often others who are walking with Him to help guide us to Him.

Reflections

Many things can keep us from surrendering our lives to Christ. We may have a poor image of ourselves based on a spirit of rejection, or feel shame because of abuse, also causing us to feel unworthy and unloved or unlovable. If you have surrendered to Christ and there were lies like these or many possible others you believed, what made you finally step out and receive the forgiveness and love of Christ so you could finally be free? _____

_____

_____

Do you believe you had a distorted image of yourself that hindered you from hearing or receiving the truth about who He says you are? _____ If so, has that image changed? How do you see yourself now?_____

_____

_____

_____

If you haven't surrendered your life to Christ, what is holding you back? Do you feel unworthy, or believe the lie that God couldn't love you? _____

_____

Do you think you would have to give up too much and it wouldn't be worth it? _____

_____

Do you have trust issues causing you to doubt that God can or will do anything to make your life better? _____ If none of the above-mentioned scenarios fits what you believe is holding you back, write what you think is your greatest hindrance._____

_____

_____

•

What do you feel is keeping you from being set free from the burdens that are weighing you down and from receiving eternal life? _____

_____

Do you not realize, apart from Christ, our lives are hopeless?_____

Apply it to Your Life

If you feel insignificant and empty, instead of running from Christ, you should run to Him. It's "Christ in you, the Hope of Glory!"

It's only through what Jesus did on the Cross that we were even able to be joined back to the Father because sin separated us from Him in the Garden of Eden. His life and body were sacrificed to make a way of escape from death, hell, and the grave, for all who would receive Him as Lord and Savior. Therefore, on that fateful day, when we stand before the Father, we can hear, "Well done, good and faithful servant," instead of, "Depart from Me, you workers of lawlessness, I never knew you!"

He truly has the final Word that will determine our eternal destiny, but it all depends on what we do before His judgment is pronounced. Deny Him, or accept His forgiveness and grace by confessing our sins and need for Him in our lives. He loves us so much, that He even warns us ahead of time. Otherwise, Jesus never would have come and died, and He would have poured His anger and wrath out on the whole world, and no one would be saved.

"For what is our hope, or joy, or crown of rejoicing? Is it not even you in the presence of our Lord Jesus Christ at His coming?"

1 Thessalonians 2:19

"To them God willed to make known what are the riches of the glory of this mystery among the Gentiles: which is Christ in you, the hope of glory."

Colossians 1:27

"God, who made the world and everything in it, since He is Lord of heaven and earth, does not dwell in temples made with hands. Nor is he worshiped with men's hands, as though He needed anything, since He gives to all life, breath, and all things. And He has made from one blood every nation of men to dwell on all the face of the earth, and has determined their preappointed times and the boundaries of their dwellings, so that they should seek the Lord, in the hope that they might grope for Him and find Him, though He is not far from each one of us; for in Him we live and move and have our being, also some of your own poets have said, 'For we are also His offspring.' Therefore, since we are the offspring of God, we ought not to think that the Divine Nature is like gold or silver or stone, something shaped by art and man's devising. Truly, these times of ignorance God overlooked, but now commands all men everywhere to repent, because He has appointed a day on which He will judge the world in righteousness by the Man whom He has ordained. He has given assurance of this to all by raising Him from the dead."

Acts 17:24-31

Notes

Salvation, Deliverance, and Freedom

A Light Will Shine

Highlights

- God's light shines even in the darkness.
- If you only see darkness and feel hopeless, then you might want to question if you truly know Him.
- The assurance of our salvation needs to be settled deep within our hearts.
- Ask Him to show you and give assurance, if you're not sure you're saved.
- If after you've asked Him to help you, you're still not sure, then ask Him to come into your heart and redeem you.
- If you are truly His, you will no longer want to willfully sin. If you slip up, quickly ask Him to forgive you and to help you not to stumble.

Reflections

Do you recall any obvious changes that took place after you prayed to receive Jesus as your Lord and Savior? Maybe you experienced an overwhelming sense of His peace and love, or maybe things (especially colors) appeared more vivid or clear. You might have felt a joy you had never felt before. Describe some things you remember, and reflect on these things as a reminder of His transforming power through His endless love for you. _____

_____

_____

Apply it to Your Life

There is truly nothing like experiencing the power and presence of our loving Creator. When we willingly invite Him into our hearts, and He enters us, then for the first time in our lives, we truly come to life! It's like we've been dead all of these years, and then we are awakened by Holy Ghost CPR (Christ Power and Resurrection). He awakens our spirits and our souls and seals us with His Spirit as He permanently comes to dwell within our spirits.

There are different phases of the Christian walk and we all grow differently in our relationships with God. The hungrier we are to truly know Him, the quicker our lives will change. If you know something changed in your heart when you had your encounter with Christ, or you simply asked Him to come into your heart, then most likely you had a true salvation experience. Having an encounter with God does not necessarily mean we will feel or experience His presence, as salvation comes by faith. You ask with a repentant heart, and you receive! Yes, He can and often will manifest His presence in us, but if He doesn't, it doesn't mean your experience wasn't real.

This is the whole reason Jesus died on the cross. So that we could be with Him and our Heavenly Father throughout eternity. Once our spirit man is born again, He begins living, moving, and having His being within us by His Spirit.

Often things do not always unfold for us as stated above, we still have our free will to get past. Ultimately we choose to let Him in or keep Him out. If we choose not to receive Him, we will never know what we are missing. We will never know true peace or our true purpose for being born. We will forever be separated from all of His grace and blessings and will walk in spiritual and eternal darkness. Our souls will never be satisfied.

If we would only surrender and trust God, He would prove His faithfulness to His Word and promises to us. Then His light will shine on us and in us, forever and ever!

"Oh, send out Your light and Your truth! Let them lead me; Let them bring me to Your holy hill and to Your tabernacle."

Psalms 43:3

"Therefore He says: "'Awake, you who sleep, Arise from the dead, And Christ will give you light.'"

Ephesians 5:14

"The entrance of Your words gives light; It gives understanding to the simple."

Psalms 119:130

"For You will light my lamp; The Lord my God will enlighten my darkness."

Psalms 18:28

Notes

Do You Know The Resurrection

Highlights

- You can be dead and still breathe.
- Being born again is a life beyond what the "natural mind" can imagine. It's a life of peace and purpose.
- God created us to need Him.
- Jesus is the only way to God the Father.
- We are eternal souls; the choice to spend eternity in Heaven or hell is solely ours.
- To reject Jesus is to choose eternal damnation.
- Repeating a "sinners prayer" is not a free ticket to Heaven, if you did not truly change in your heart.
- Choosing Christ is the best decision you will ever make in your entire life.

Reflections

Have you ever been dead and brought back to life; physically or spiritually? _____

If yes, describe your experience. _____

_____

_____

Does your heart feel numb and empty, as if you have no purpose? _____

If so, then you could be spiritually dead, and only physically alive. To be spiritually dead is to have no connection with God or Jesus. Until you cry out to Him to save your soul, He is not obligated to hear your prayers. We are a spirit, we have a soul—our mind, will, and emotions—and we live in a body.

Have you ever prayed a "sinners prayer" with a pastor, evangelist, or someone else, just because you were asked to repeat after them?_____

If yes, were you praying with a heart of repentance; sorry and broken for your sin? Or because you felt pressured to pray, so you would "fit in" and not be condemned or shunned? Or maybe another reason?_____

_____

_____

Apply it to Your Life

Without Jesus on the throne of our hearts, we're not much different than a body in a grave (where our purpose is concerned). God created us with purpose and until we call out to Him with a heart that is broken for our sin and rebellion against Him, we will never fulfill our purpose for being born. When your physical body does quit functioning and you pass from this life, if you have not chosen to call out to Him, then it will be too late. You will spend eternity completely separated from Him, in outer darkness, being tormented by the very one who deceived you and made you believe you didn't need Jesus. If you prayed a "sinner's prayer" without a heart convicted and broken for your sin, then you might as well be whispering in the wind. Without the right heart, saying a "sinner's prayer" will not save you any more than standing in a garage will make you a car. God, your Creator, knows your heart and the intentions of your heart. If you truly did not have a heart desiring to change, He knows; you can't fool God.

If you are sick and tired of being sick and tired, and you desire to see your life change, call out to Jesus. Tell Him you're sorry for your sin and rebellion, ask Him to save your soul and to fill your heart with His Spirit.

Jesus died on the cross to save us from our sins and to set us free from the curse of sin we were born with. Because He is the Son of God who came to the earth to break the power of sin over us, He was without sin but became sin for us. He was the ultimate sacrifice for all mankind. There is no other way to be saved. He is the only way to the Father. If, when we stand before God on judgment day, we want to hear, "Well done good and faithful servant," and not "Depart from Me, worker of lawlessness, I never knew you!" We must call on His name.

Choosing Christ Jesus is by far the best decision you will ever make in your life. It will take you right into His presence, into eternity forevermore. If you haven't made this life-changing decision, please don't delay any longer. We are not guaranteed our next breath. Receive the "gift of life," then watch Him transform your life in ways you never imagined He would or could. With a sincere heart, repent and surrender all of your pain, cares, torment, and junk to Him, then taste and see that the Lord is good.

Jesus said to him, "I am the way, the truth, and the life. No one comes to the Father except through Me."

John 14:6

Jesus said to her, "I am the resurrection and the life. He who believes in Me, though he may die, he shall live."

John 11:25

"I, even I, am the Lord, And besides Me there is no savior."

Isaiah 43:11

Notes

Don't Let Your Heart Be Troubled

Highlights

- Troubled times are here. There has never been a time in our lives that evil has been so rampant.
- The earth is shaking. The atmosphere is full of all sorts of activities—many strange phenomena.
- Governments are corrupt, news media are out of control, not reporting the news as it happens.
- There are times and seasons for all things.
- With God, there is hope through Jesus.
- These are the last days, the time to call on the name of Jesus is running out. Don't put it off any longer.
- Connect with a strong believer if you have questions you can't find the answers to. Read the Bible (either the physical book or on a Bible App.) Seek Him and you will find Him.

Reflections

When you see all that is happening in the world, what are you feeling: scared, anxious, unsure about what to do or who you can trust, or many different emotions? _____

_____

_____

Are you filled with more questions than answers? _____

Or, do you have peace in the turmoil? _____

Do you have the assurance, beyond the shadow of a doubt, that no matter what happens, you are protected and cared for in the loving hands of your Heavenly Father? _____

_____

_____

Apply it to Your Life

We are no doubt living in uncertain times. If you're feeling restless, fearful, or unsure of how to move forward, or which way to turn, rest assured, God loves you so much that He made it a point to get this (His) book in your hands. It's not His will that anyone should perish. However, we are living in the last days, my friends. We must choose now.

If you are paying attention to the signs around us, you know the earth is groaning. Most prophecies have been fulfilled, with many events taking place as I write. As the signs of the times are unfolding all around us, Jesus' soon return is immenant for those who are prepared to join Him.

I beckon you, if you have read this far and are still on the fence about your eternal destiny, if you have not called out to Jesus to save your soul and to forgive you for your sins, you are about to run out of time. Today is the day of salvation. He longs to be reunited with His children.

Don't let fear or pride, through the voice and lies of the enemy stop you from walking in the freedom of the cross. Jesus died so you can live. He was resurrected and ascended to Heaven to sit at the right hand of the Father. He has been long awaiting His return to receive those who chose to call on His name, to take them to their eternal home to be with Him.

No man knows the day or the hour of His return (not even Him), only God the Father knows (Matthew 24:36). The Word says, "He will come in the twinkling of an eye" (1 Corinthians 15:52). That is faster than you can blink!

Let go of all of your inhibitions and doubts and receive by faith your salvation today. Faith is to trust that God will do what He promises. "He is not a man that He should lie" (Numbers 23:19). If He says He will do something, then you can 100% be sure that it will be done.

God is our only hope through Jesus, His only begotten Son. Eternal light is His promise to all who receive Him. Eternal darkness and torment is His promise to all who reject Him. What do you choose? Light or darkness?

"The earth is violently broken, The earth is split open, The earth is shaken exceedingly."

Isaiah 24:19

"Our help is in the name of the Lord, Who made heaven and earth."

Psalms 124:8

"But of that day and hour no one knows, not even the angels of heaven, but My Father only."

Matthew 24:36 (Spoken by Jesus)

"Behold, I tell you a mystery: We shall not all sleep, but we shall all be changed—in a moment, in the twinkling of an eye, at the last trumpet. For the trumpet will sound, and the dead will be raised incorruptible, and we shall be changed."

1 Corinthians 15:51-52

"To everything there is a season, A time to every purpose under heaven: A time to be born, And a time to die; A time to plant, And a time to pluck what is planted; A time to kill, And a time to heal; A time to break down, And a time to build up; A time to weep, And a time to laugh; A time to mourn, And a time to dance; A time to cast away stones, And a time to gather stones; A time to embrace, And a time to refrain from embracing; A time to gain, And a time to lose; A time to keep, and a time to throw away; A time to tear, And a time to sew; A time to keep silence, And a time to speak; A time to love, And a time to hate; A time of war, And a time of peace."

Ecclesiastes 3:1-8

Notes

He Who Promised Is Faithful

Highlights

- No matter what God promises, we can be sure He will fulfill His promises— either promises for hope (blessings) or promises for judgment (curses).
- Just knowing about God does not assure you of His hope and peace. But, it could assure you of His judgment.
- For assurance of His hope and your eternal destiny to be secure, you should have intimate fellowship with Him through reading the Word and spending time in prayer daily.
- Without the blood Jesus shed when He died on the cross, we would all perish in our sin without hope, eternally separating us from God.
- By not choosing to walk in God's promises, you are choosing to walk in His judgment. To choose Him means you receive Him as Lord and Savior of your life as you repent of your sins and turn away from them.
- Nobody was meant to spend eternity in hell. It was made for satan and his minions, not for anybody else.

Reflections

Have you ever received a promise or promises from God? _____

Were they promises of blessings or curses or both? _____

If you are born again, what are some of the obvious things you've noticed that changed about you when you accepted Jesus as your Savior?_____
_____
_____

If you don't know Jesus as your Savior, are there changes you have tried to make happen on your own but you just can't make them happen? Maybe you're addicted to drugs, alcohol, sex, food; maybe you swear all the time and can't seem to stop, or you're controlling or critical of others, impatient, headstrong, etc.—you fill in the blanks.
_____
_____

Apply it to Your Life

If you've received Jesus as your Lord and Savior, you received the greatest and most rewarding promise ever given by God—the assurance of salvation through the blood of His One and Only Son. This is His eternal promise for those who are born again.

We may, however, live a life that seems to be filled with blessings, often as a result of others' prayers; God honors the prayers of His children if they are prayed in faith. So, there may be some you know (or even you yourself) who have not made a personal commitment to walk with Jesus, yet seem to be blessed and don't feel the need to make any change, seeing no purpose in it.

If you do not know Jesus as your Savior, you are carnally minded. You are only seeking after the desires of your flesh. To be carnally minded leads to death and eternal separation from God. To be spiritually minded is to be a child of God and to have the heart of God within you, which leads to eternal life. You desire to live a life that is holy and pleasing to Him, no longer looking to satisfy the sinful nature of the flesh.

This transformation happens when we realize the emptiness and lack in our lives. Not lack of material things, but lack of being complete. The only way we will ever walk free and complete is by calling on the name of Jesus and repenting of our sins. Then, the burden for change is on Him, not you. He knows if your heart is sincere and if you were truly broken over your sin. With a desire to live for Him and no longer for yourself, He will transform you instantly. You will know beyond a shadow of a doubt that something has changed inside of you. But then, the transformation process continues as you walk in your new-found freedom in Christ.

Do you truly know Him, or just know about Him? If you just know about Him, don't let the enemy rob you of God's temporal and eternal blessings. Satan will do anything in his power to keep you from walking in the blessings and promises of God. He is a liar and is very convincing in his lies. When you truly know God, you are complete and set up to finish the race of the High Calling of Christ. You will grow in your relationship with Him and walk in His grace and blessings. You will no longer want to live like the old you because you are now "a new creation in Christ."

"For to be carnally minded is death, but to be spiritually minded is life and peace."

Romans 8:6

"And do not be conformed to this world, but be transformed by the renewing of your mind, that you may prove what is that good and acceptable and perfect will of God."

Romans 12:2

"Therefore, if anyone is in Christ, he is a new creation; old things have passed away; behold, all things have become new."

2 Corinthians 5:17

Notes

Holy Spirit Help Those Who Are Hurting Learn How To Trust You

Highlights

- Most everyone suffers pain as they grow up—often betrayal, rejection, neglect, violation, abuse, lies, and deceit. None of us come through life unscathed.
- You should be able to trust those who are often the ones who hurt you the most. This is typically because a spirit of iniquity has passed down through the generations.
- Due to the pain many suffer as children or even adults, they learn to put their guard up and find it nearly impossible to put their trust in others.
- Sometimes those severely wounded may think they know God, but their understanding of who God is is skewed. It's based on the "role models" they had growing up, causing them to have a disfigured image of who God truly is.
- He sent His Son to set free those who are bound and held captive because of the lies and deception of the enemy.
- The very One we are avoiding and unwilling to trust is the One who can break those chains off us and fill us with His love.
- Only God can change our hearts and cause us to see His goodness. Those things that were passed down from your ancestors can be broken and no longer allowed to move into future generations.
- God has a plan and purpose for our lives different from what most of us grew up thinking about. If we're not walking with Him, we will never know His plans or all we're supposed to accomplish.

Reflections

If you are a Child of God and you believe beyond a shadow of a doubt you're going to spend eternity with Him, is there anyone who has deeply hurt you that you have not yet forgiven or felt like you could forgive?

_____

_____

Do you feel that God is distant and doesn't care about the pain you've suffered? _____

_____

_____

Are you mad at God for allowing this or these things to happen to you? _____
(It's okay to admit it; He already knows what's in your heart.)

Apply it to Your Life

As I already stated, we all suffer something or many things in our lives, as we are products of a fallen world. But, because of this fallen world we live in, we have an Advocate to help us. Jesus came to be the One who unites us back to the Father by forgiving us of our sins. As God has forgiven us, when we receive Him as our Lord and Savior, we must forgive others to continue to receive the forgiveness of our Father.

God knows all we have suffered, and He knows our hearts about these things and towards the offender(s). His Word says; "But if you do not forgive, neither will your Father in heaven forgive your trespasses (sins)" (Mark 11:26).

If you've been violated, abused, or victimized in any way, you have had your trust breached. You may feel you have a right to be angry and to hold resentment towards anyone who has wronged you. But holding on to this resentment is not benefiting you at all. It is being used as a weapon of the enemy against you to bring you more agony and pain. He knows what God's Word says about forgiveness, and he is most likely speaking things to you to cause you to justify the hardness in your heart.

God's Word says, "Vengeance is Mine, I will repay," says the Lord (Romans 12:19). This means, as we are obedient to forgive those who have hurt us, we will be forgiven by God. They will have to answer to God for the wrongs they've done to us or anyone else. We will each have to stand before God and answer to Him one day, so nobody gets away with anything they've done that isn't covered under the blood of Jesus. In other words, if we have not been washed and cleansed by the blood of Jesus through repentance and forgiveness, then we will stand before God in judgment. But, if we have been forgiven through repentance and cleansed from our sins, then when we stand before the Father, we will be exonerated and approved to enter the Kingdom of Heaven. This means we were guilty, just like the one who was judged, but because we chose to walk with Jesus and to repent and to continually repent as needed, then we are cleared from all wrongdoing, ever.

Even if the person has already passed, or is still alive, in your life, or no longer in your life, it is crucial to forgive them, no matter how hard or impossible it may seem. If forgiving others was impossible, God would not have instructed us to do so. If He tells us to do something, then He will always give us the grace to do it.

Also, sometimes when we choose to forgive someone, we still have a hard time and don't feel we have forgiveness towards them. It first has to come as a decision. You have to choose to do it. Then, ask God for the grace to forgive them for what they did. As you humble yourself and admit to God that you are struggling and need His help, He will honor your willingness to obey and will help you. You may have to walk through this process many times before you finally know you have fully released them to God, and the pain of the offense is no longer stinging you. Ask God to forgive you for harboring bitterness and resentment in your heart, and then ask Him to heal your heart and emotions from whatever took place. He is waiting to take the pain away and even erase the memory if you ask Him to.

Because we live in a fallen world, God does not cause bad things to happen to us. We were all born with free will, and He does not control us like we're robots. There is evil all around us. Though the enemy controls the thoughts and actions of many, what satan meant for evil, God can turn around for our good. If you're mad at God, tell Him and ask Him where He was as your abuse was taking place. Then listen and see what you sense Him telling you. He is always close to the brokenhearted.

"But if you do not forgive, neither will your Father in heaven forgive your trespasses."

Mark 11:26

"Beloved, do not avenge yourselves, but rather give place to wrath; for it is written, "Vengeance is Mine, I will repay." says the Lord."

Romans 12:19

"Would not God search this out? For He knows the secrets of the heart."

Psalms 44:21

"The Lord is near to those who have a broken heart, And saves such as have a contrite spirit."

Psalms 34:18

Notes

Lord, Please Open My Eyes

Highlights

- Some things can hinder us from walking in God's grace, and we may not be aware of them.
- Often we are dealing with weaknessess of the flesh that cause us to continue in bad habits.
- More so, we are dealing with iniquities that have been passed down through our bloodline. These are also known as generational curses.
- The enemy is constantly coming against us, speaking lies and keeping us bound in sin, doubt, and unbelief—always trying to entice us to do things that will keep us separated from God.
- We need to also lift our families in prayer, as they too can suffer the same weaknesses we have suffered because of the enemy's strongholds over families.
- As we grow stronger in our Christian walk, we can share the hope we have with others who have no hope. We become stronger as we share our hope with others.
- Always give thanks to Jesus for setting us free through His shed blood on the cross.

Reflections

What are some of the things you feel could be hindering you from walking in God's grace and blessings? Just a few examples that may get you thinking are pride, rebellion and disobedience, anger, unforgiveness, resentment, the need to be in control, shyness, stubbornness, feelings of rejection, self-hatred, and many more. (Many of these are forms of pride.) You may already know some things, but pray also and ask God to reveal to you anything that you haven't thought of or anything not mentioned above. List each thing that comes to mind even if you have to go to a separate sheet of paper for more space. _____

_____

_____

_____

_____

Generational curses are curses/iniquities that are passed down from your ancestors (parents, grandparents, etc.). They are strongholds from the enemy. You may have spirits of lust or sexual perversion, rejection, anger, depression, fear, murder, insanity, physical ailments or diseases, bondage to any stronghold, such as addictions as mentioned above, and the list goes on.

Are there any iniquities/generational curses that you can see were passed down to you? You may have always just said, "I'm just like my mother, or just like my father," and in a sense this is true, as you inherit physical and physiological characteristics of your ancestors through your DNA, but you can also inherit their iniquities through the generational curses. What are some things you can see that may have been passed down through your generational bloodline?_____

_____

_____

What are some of the lies the enemy speaks to you that keeps you from believing God? Anything that you hear as a thought that contradicts the Word of God is a lie from the enemy. You may hear that you're ugly, you're pitiful, unlovable, a failure who will never amount to anything; you're weird, slow, stupid, too fat, too thin, poor, talk too much, you get the point. List all of the lies you can think of and ask God to reveal any others to you._____

_____

_____

_____

_____

Apply it to Your Life

The only way we can dispel the lies of the enemy and no longer let them have power to control us is to counteract it with the Word of God. God's Word is the only foundation we have that is safe to stand on. It is the only truth and will strengthen you as you commit to reading it and learning how to use it in prayer and in standing against the enemy when he is coming against your thoughts.

"For I the Lord your God, am a jealous God, visiting the iniquity of the fathers upon the children to the third and fourth generations of those who hate Me."

Exodus 20:5

"I call heaven and earth as witnesses today against you, that I have set before you life and death, blessing and cursing; therefore choose life, that both you and your descendants may live."

Deuteronomy 30:19

"The thief does not come except to steal, and to kill, and to destroy. I have come that they may have life, and that they may have it more abundantly."

John 10:10

Now that you've gone through this Journal page and made your list of the things requested above, take your list and place it before the Father. Go back to the prayer written in the devotional with the same title as this one (Lord, Please Open My Eyes), and pray it out loud to The Father. Release these things to Him and ask Him to help you to be quick to repent and to let go of anything that is stopping you from walking in His fullness.

Notes

New Home And Job Loss Testimony

Highlights

- No matter what the future holds, we have nothing to worry about if we know Who holds the future.
- Life changes are inevitable. We may perceive them as bad, causing us to worry unnecessarily about something out of our control. Only God has the full picture and knows best why things happen as they do. We just need to trust His plans.
- Moving is not always easy, but it sure is a good time to purge things you no longer need.
- Remember, when you help others in their time of need, you are sowing seed. When you sow into others' lives, it will always come back to you, so make sure what you're sowing is good seed.
- When God closes one door, He will open another.
- Be ready to embrace the new chapters God has for you.

Reflections

Do you truly know the God of hope, Creator of the Universe, the Lover of your soul, or do you just know about Him? If you only know about Him and you don't know Him intimately, you are missing out on so much. If you only knew how much He loves you and the amazing plans He has for your life. No one can fathom or grasp the beauty and wonder of God's plans for their lives. The Bible says if we draw closer to God, He will draw closer to us. He doesn't force Himself on us, but He longs to have fellowship with us.

Are there things you can think of that you could change to allow yourself to spend more time seeking God through prayer and reading His Word?_____

_____

_____

Maybe you could set aside a certain time during your day just for Him. Reading the Word, praying, and worshiping Him are the only ways to get acquainted with Him. Perhaps you can cut out some things that may not be of real significance to you, such as watching TV, spending time on social media, playing video games, going shopping, playing sports, or doing anything else excessively that robs you of time.

Think about things you can do, then make a list of how you can dedicate special time to getting acquainted with The Father._____

_____

_____

What was a major change you had to make in your life you may have perceived as bad, but it turned out to be good? _____

_____

_____

What was your initial reaction to this change taking place? Fear, anger, confusion, joy, or something else? _____

_____

_____

What are some ways you can make a positive difference in others' lives? _____

_____

_____

Apply it to Your Life

As I stated, life is full of changes. If we are so set in our ways that we can't embrace change, we will miss out on so many of the blessings that God has for our lives. He created us with a much higher purpose than what we could ever imagine. If we are resistant to changes He is bringing about in our lives, we may never know what His purpose is for our lives. We could fall short of His call for us as we somehow think we know better than Him, the One who has the power to save our souls or to condemn us to hell.

"For I know the plans I have for you," declares the Lord. "plans to prosper you and not to harm you, plans to give you hope and a future. Then you will call on me and come and pray to me, and I will listen to you. You will seek me and find me when you seek me with all of your heart."

Jeremiah 29:11-13 (NIV)

"Therefore, whatever you want men to do to you, do also to them, for this is the Law and the Prophets." (Do unto others what you would have them do unto you).

Matthew 7:12

"Draw near to God and He will draw near to you. Cleanse your hands, you sinners; and purify your hearts, you double-minded."

James 4:8

Notes

Ready Or Not, He's Coming Soon

Highlights

- Many people are living their lives as if they have all of the time in the world. Jesus will be returning soon, and if He is not made Lord of their lives, it will be too late for them.
- Saying a "sinner's prayer" has given many people false hope that they are secure in their salvation. Unless there is a true conviction of your sin and a heart change, saying a "sinner's prayer" is not enough to get you into heaven or to save you from the judgment of God.
- So many things are happening in the world now that point to His soon return.
- God's heart is for none to perish in their sin. Call out to Him before it's too late.
- Those walking in darkness are separating more and more from those who are walking in His light. As His return grows closer, the darkness will grow even darker and the light will grow brighter.
- Those walking with Christ are walking in their God-given purpose—loving Him, loving others, and sharing the hope that they have with those who have no hope.
- We're not guaranteed our next breath; don't wait until you hear, "Depart from me, I never knew you." It will be too late.

Reflections

Are you living your life with anticipation of Jesus' return, or are you living as if you have all the time in the world with no thought of His return? _____

_____

_____

Did you say a "sinner's prayer" and now think you're safe from God's judgment, thinking everything is okay? ___

_____

_____

If things didn't change after praying the "sinner's prayer," and you're still living your life as before; if you're not praying, reading the Word, or worshiping God daily, then you may not have had a true salvation experience.

These are hard questions and many may feel they're being judged, but it is better to ask the hard questions now than to wait until it's too late. There is no judgment here, only a challenge to search your heart.

If you've questioned your salvation and feel it is unsettled, call out to God. Ask Him to show you the truth. Repent of anything that you are shown that may be stumbling blocks in your life and release them to the Father.

Do you still enjoy doing things that you did before you prayed? _____

Are you willing to compromise in situations that God states in His Word is sin? _____

_____

Do you believe fudging (compromising) just a little bit is okay? _____

Apply it to Your Life

If you think it is okay to compromise even a little bit, search your heart. When you truly surrender your heart to God, that is exactly what you're doing. You give up your will and seek His will. It's not something that should be a struggle at all. Your heart's desires change, and it is something you long to do to please Him. He does not want any of us to perish, but if our hearts aren't sold out to Him, then the likelihood of us spending eternity with Him is slim.

"Now the works of the flesh are evident, which are: adultery, fornication, uncleanness, lewdness, idolatry, sorcery, hatred, contentions, jealousies, outbursts of wrath, selfish ambitions, dissensions, heresies, envy, murders, drunkenness, revelries, and the like; of which I tell you beforehand, just as I also told you in time past, that those who practice such things will not inherit the kingdom of God."

Galatians 5:19-21

"But the fruit of the Spirit is love, joy, peace, longsuffering, kindness, goodness, faithfulness, gentleness, self-control. Against such there is no law. And those who are Christ's have crucified the flesh with its passions and desires. If we live in the Spirit, let us also walk in the Spirit. Let us not become conceited, provoking one another, envying one another."

Galatians 5:22-26

"And then I will declare to them, 'I never knew you; depart from Me, you who practice lawlessness!'"

Matthew 7:23

"His lord said to him, 'Well done, good and faithful servant; you have been faithful over a few things, I will make you ruler over many things. Enter into the joy of your lord.'"

Matthew 25:23

"These things I have spoken to you, that My joy may remain in you, and that your joy may be full."

John 15:11

Notes

The Good Shepherd

Highlights

- Just as a shepherd of sheep looks after his flock, when we are God's children, He too looks after us. He leads us and guides us.
- When we go astray, He will always do whatever we allow Him do to lead us back to Him.
- The enemy does not like losing someone to God who was living for him. He will use the things he knows are weaknesses in you to try to lure you away from your Father. Just as God does, he will do whatever you allow him do to win you back. If he's successful, before long, you will start feeling bitter and angry inside towards others or even God, which will lead you deeper into sin.
- When we cry out to God with a broken and repentant heart, He will receive us back to Him. He will use His rod and staff to bring correction and comfort to us.
- When you pray for God to forgive you, even if you've prayed before, when your heart is sincere, He will not turn you away. He longs to have fellowship with us and to care for us.
- Your heart's cry needs to be one desiring to have a deep relationship with Him. One who longs to know His heart intimately. As you cry out to Him, He will wash you and cleanse you fresh and new. Making you a spotless lamb.

Reflections

Are you walking with the Lord, knowing His hand is upon your life guiding you down the path you need to be walking on?_____

Is there a time that you turned away from God and knew He was trying to get your attention to come back to Him?_____

If yes, what do you feel was the reason you turned away from Him? Needing to grow more in your relationship with Him through reading the Word and spending time in prayer? _____Feeling weak and unable to resist temptations?_____ Feeling confused and unsure of who you are in Christ? _____Did you take offense towards someone or even God? _____

Maybe there are other reasons you can list? _____
_____
_____

What are some weaknesses you know you have that the enemy might try to lure you back into?_____
_____
_____

Is there any specific time you can think of that God either brought correction to you or He brought comfort to you? If so, what was it, and how did it make you feel?_____

_____

_____

Apply it to Your Life

If you feel you're separated from God in any way, please refer back to the poem with the same title (The Good Shepherd) in the devotional, and read it again with a heart of repentance and trust that He will continue to pour His love out on you as you humble yourself before Him.

"The Lord is my shepherd; I shall not want. He makes me to lie down in green pastures; He leads me beside the still waters. He restores my soul; He leads me in the paths of righteousness for His name's sake. Yea, though I walk through the valley of the shadow of death I will fear no evil; For You are with me; Your rod and Your staff, they comfort me. You prepare a table before me in the presence of my enemies; You anoint my head with oil; My cup runs over. Surely goodness and mercy shall follow me all the days of my life; And I will dwell in the house of the Lord forever."

Psalms 23:1-6

Notes

Do You Truly Know Him?

Highlights

- Know Him through reading His Word.
- Trust Him and give Him thanksgiving and praise for His blessings.
- When Jesus loves you, you can love you.
- When you truly know Him, your life is transformed.
- Without Jesus, we are powerless to live a transformed life.

Reflections

Do you remember having a life-transforming, salvation experience where you met Jesus by the power of the Holy Spirit?_____

_____

_____

If so, describe as best you can what took place. (Did you feel God's tangible presence? If so, were you moved to tears by His presence, or did you feel scared or unsure about what took place? Maybe you felt peace, joy, hope, or loved unconditionally.) _____

_____

_____

Do you have a hunger for reading the Word and getting to know Him more intimately now? _____

_____

_____

Do you see yourself differently than you did before surrendering your heart to Jesus?_____ Do you love the person you see in the mirror, or do you still struggle with things that hinder you from seeing yourself as Jesus sees you?_____

_____

Apply it to Your Life

These are not definitive criteria to specifically say you were or were not born again but could be a gauge to help you reflect on your experience then or your relationship now. If you do not desire a deeper walk with God but want one, ask Him to stir that hunger in you. Ask Him to show you anything you need to surrender (repent of) that could hinder your walk. Pray daily—often, read the Bible, give Him praise and worship for saving and using you for His glory. He will use you to show others His love if you desire Him to.

If you struggle to love the person you see in the mirror, then you may want to call out to Jesus and ask Him what's keeping you from seeing yourself the way He sees you. If you are struggling with shame, self-loathing, and self-hate, possibly due to some abuse in your past, then it may be hard to feel love for yourself. Often, someone who has suffered abuse internalizes their pain and blames themselves for what happened to them.

The abuser can also cause this internalization by telling you that if you had not done this or had done that, this wouldn't be happening and that it is all your fault. These are all lies from the pit of hell. They were being used as a vessel of darkness to destroy you by the enemy of your soul, satan.

If you want freedom from this pain and torment, one thing you must do is forgive your abuser. That sounds like an impossible task, but our freedom comes through forgiveness. If God instructs us to forgive others, He will give us the grace to do so as we trust Him. Just as when you prayed for Jesus to come into your heart through forgiveness, we must also release forgiveness to those who have wronged us. If we can't forgive, God can't set us free. If God doesn't forgive us, we will always be bound and in darkness.

Once we surrender our abusers to God and let go of the bitterness in our hearts, the chains that were keeping us bound no longer have the power to hold us from walking in freedom. Then the person we see in the mirror is someone we can love and is worthy of receiving His love. Pure Agape love is our Father's love for us. There is none other like it, as it is pure and holy.

"Now by this we know that we know Him, if we keep His commandments. He who says, "I know Him," and does not keep His commandments, is a liar, and the truth is not in him. But whoever keeps His word, truly the love of God is perfected in him. By this we know that we are in Him. He who says he abides in Him ought himself also to walk just as He walked."

1 John 2:3-6

"But if you do not forgive, neither will your Father in heaven forgive your trespasses."

Mark 11:26

Notes

Final Thoughts

Congratulations on completing the reading of this Spirit inspired book and journal. Not only did the Holy Spirit inspire this writing, He also inspired you to read it and to search your heart and His too! It is His desire for all to know Him and seek to live in His perfect will for our lives. The only way we can be successful at living in His will is to truly know Him.

As your wisdom, understanding and insight increases through your personal journey and walk with the Lord, you will feel (and know) that you are more acquainted with Him as He is with you. You will have a greater connection to His Spirit and you will discover you are hearing and obeying His still small voice more clearly. This is when you will know, Yes, I truly know Him, and no longer just know about Him.

You will never fully know Him because there are too many facets in Him to know, but you will always be stirred to know Him more. You will become bolder as you long to share this hope in you with others. You will stand in your God given authority as you come against principalities, powers, and rulers of darkness in heavenly places; as you lay hands on the sick, raise the dead, and cast out demons; as you break the chains of oppression off of those who are bound.

When you truly know Him, you will finally start to understand your God given purpose for being born. You will become a vessel of His light in the earth and be used to set the captive free, so they too can learn to truly know Him and not just know about Him.

By serving our earthly purpose for being born; through doing all that is mentioned above, and even more, then we (all who are His children; blood bought and redeemed through Jesus) will come to our eternal purpose for being born; to forever and ever worship The King of kings, and Lord or lords, The Great I AM, The Alpha and Omega, our Creator, The Author and Finisher of our faith. We will forever worship Him with all of the angels and saints that have gone before us throughout all eternity.

To God be all of the Glory, all of the Honor, and all of the Praise, FOREVER AND EVER!
I am honored and humbled to be His servant and vessel, I thank you, and God above, for each one He stirs to read His book, *Do You Truly Know Him*.

In His Most Holy Name,
Matcine Pepper